Proclamation and Theology

HORIZONS IN THEOLOGY

Proclamation and Theology

WILLIAM H. WILLIMON

Abingdon Press
Nashville

PROCLAMATION AND THEOLOGY

Copyright © 2005 by Abingdon Press

This book is printed on acid-free paper.

Library of Congress Cataloging-in-Publication Data

Willimon, William H.
  Proclamation and theology / William H. Willimon.
     p. cm.—(Horizons in theology)
  ISBN 0-687-49343-9 (alk. paper)
  1. Preaching. I. Title. II. Series.

  BV4211.3.W53 2005
  251—dc22

                                                              2005008948

05 06 07 08 09 10 11 12 13 14—10 9 8 7 6 5 4 3 2 1

MANUFACTURED IN THE UNITED STATES OF AMERICA

CONTENTS

INTRODUCTION

*Now those who were scattered went from place to place,
proclaiming the word. (Acts 8:4)*

This is the first thing said about the church after the bloody death of Stephen, the church's first martyr. A terrible persecution was launched against the church after Stephen's death, with women and men being dragged from their homes, imprisoned, and killed. The authorities are determined once and for all to bring an end to the Jesus commotion. And what do the disciples do? They preach. They explode into the world with their speaking. Amid a bloody persecution of the church, one might think that the church would keep its head down, keep quiet, bow in deferential silence before the murderous assault of the authorities, hide out until the trouble blows over. But these are Christians and they talk a lot, go public, talk to anyone who will listen, talk even when their talk brings out the worst in their neighbors, talk even when no one listens.

You may take this as a useful thumbnail summary definition of the church and its mission: "Now those who were scattered went from place to place proclaiming the word."

Something like fifty million Americans—many millions more than will go to a movie—will gather in churches this week and do something strange. They will listen to a sermon. This is one of the most peculiar of Christian activities. There are religions that practice their faith by sitting quietly in some serene surrounding and meditating. There are other faiths that cultivate acts of individual piety, ritual gestures that are designed to bring one close to God. Christianity believes that a primary way of getting close to God is by listening to a speech.

But a sermon is a speech that is more. That "more" is the purpose of this book. Preaching is a theological act, our attempt to do business with a God who speaks. It is also a theological act in that a sermon is God's attempt to do business with us through words. Most speeches that we hear require a host of skills, insights, and gifts to make them work. I have just listened to a speech by a man who was attempting to sell me a new car. His speech was quite effective because of his skillful arrangement of his argument, his apt use of the English language, and his physical presentation. Preaching at times may use all of these rhetorical devices and use them well. But none of these devices is at the heart of what preaching is up to. At the heart of preaching is either a God who speaks, and who speaks now, in the sermon, or preaching is silly.

The God who comes to us as Jesus the Christ is a garrulous God. Mark, presumably the earliest of the Gospels begins with, "Jesus came into Galilee, preaching the gospel of God, and saying, 'The time is fulfilled, and the kingdom of God is at hand; repent, and believe in the gospel'" (Mark 1:14-15 RSV). What did Jesus do for a living? "He went . . . preaching in their synagogues" (Mark 1:39 RSV). So in talking about sermons and preaching, we are talking about a communicative God. We are talking about one of the most distinctive and peculiar aspects of the God of Israel and the church—"And God said. . . ." This is the basis for preaching, and even for the Christian faith itself—a God who speaks to us and enables us to hear God's speaking.

This book is not so much about the theological content of preaching, or a theological justification for why we continue to concoct and to listen to sermons. This book is an essay, derived from my more than three decades of preaching, on preaching as a theological activity. It is based upon the conviction that preaching is not about us—not about you the listener or about me the preacher. Preaching is about God and by God, or it is silly.

This book is written from the conviction that if there is anything wrong with preaching as we know it today, what's wrong is theological. It is my judgment that contemporary homiletics has expended too much energy on issues of style, technique, rhetoric, the limits of the hearers, and the nature of the preacher. I believe that the history of Christian preaching shows that preaching is always revived and carried forth on a rising theological tide. When the messenger is grasped by a significant message, the messenger will find a way to deliver the message, and if the message is significant, God will bless the messenger's efforts. There is nothing wrong with contemporary preaching that can't be cured through having something to say about and from God.

Yet even good theology is no guarantee that our preaching will be gladly received by the multitudes. I expect that Jesus preached away more people than he won. Jonathan Edwards labored as pastor in Northampton, Massachusetts, for an uneventful seven lean years, preaching the gospel week-in-week-out with little congregational response to show for it. Then, without warning, his congregation experienced a series of what Edwards called "surprising conversions." Edwards, who is one of the greatest minds America has produced, was wonderfully befuddled by this outbreak of religious vitality. He was an incredibly dull preacher who read his sermons for hours on end, rarely looking up from his text and almost never changing the tone of his voice. In 1737 he wrote an account of the heart-warming revival that broke out among his congregation, delightfully called *A Faithful Narrative of the Surprising Work of God in the Conversion of Many Hundred Souls in Northampton, and Neighboring Towns and Villages*. I like to think that Edwards had such an understanding of the peculiarity of the gospel, coupled with an awareness of the cognitive intransigence of his people, that he was therefore genuinely surprised when anyone heard, really heard, and responded to his preaching. We ought also to be surprised.

When I emerged from seminary and began to preach, I thought that about the worst fate that could befall me as a preacher was not to be heard. It was my task, through the homiletical, rhetorical arts, to bridge the gap, the great communicative gap between speaker and listener. I now know that I had been taught to misconstrue the gap. The gap, the evangelical distance that ought to concern the preacher, is not one of time—the historical space between Jesus and us—nor is it one of communication—the rhetorical space between speaker and listener. The gap that is the main concern of the evangelical preacher, and a concern of most of this book, is the theological space between us and the Trinity. Contemporary homiletical thought has focused upon style, rhetoric, or method when *Theos* ought to be our concern. Our problem as preachers is not that we must labor to render these strange biblical stories intelligible to modern people but rather that these biblical stories render a God true but strange.

How different is this approach that begins theologically rather than rhetorically from so much of contemporary homiletics. The new genre of church-marketing books typified by the work of George Barna, church-growth strategist, tends to make preaching a mere technique for human communication rather than the divinely appointed means of God's communication with us. In his popular books, with names like *Marketing the Church* and *User Friendly Churches*, written for clergy, Barna tells us that

> Jesus Christ was a communications specialist. He communicated His message in diverse ways, and with results that would be a credit to modern advertising and marketing agencies. Notice the Lord's approach: He identified His target audience, determined their need, and delivered His message directly. . . . He promoted His product in the most efficient way possible: by communicating with the "hot prospects."
>
> Don't underestimate the marketing lessons Jesus taught. He understood His product thoroughly, developed an unparalleled distribution system, advanced a method of promotion that has penetrated every continent, and offered His product at a price that is within the grasp of every consumer (without making the product so accessible that it lost its value).[1]

This sad selling-out of Jesus is the inevitable result of equating Christian proclamation with savvy marketing strategies. The only protection against the church falling facedown in the mire of contemporary American consumerism is constant focus upon God, theology. Theology makes preaching as difficult and demanding as it ought to be. Theology tests whether or not what we preach is Christ Jesus and him crucified rather than humanity and it slightly improved.

I did something last week that I have done so often that it has now ceased to be strange. I preached a sermon. I spoke about twenty minutes upon a biblical text, using a number of illustrations, some from literature, some from current events, and some from the lives of ordinary people like me. At the conclusion of the sermon we recited a creed, sang a hymn, took up an offering, made Eucharist, and we went forth.

At the front door, as people filed out of the service, some said things like, "Nice service," or "Good sermon, preacher." But one young woman shook my hand and said, "Thanks. God really spoke to me today. I felt a presence. Thanks. I feel like I know what I've got to do next week."

I do not know precisely what happened between that young woman and God. I do not know what she heard or what she will do with what she heard. All I know is that, whatever it was, it wasn't silly. It was a surprising, holy miracle, a divine intervention quite beyond the range of my abilities or intentions. She heard the very voice of God. Her name was called. She was addressed, summoned by nothing more spectacular, but certainly nothing less miraculous, than a sermon.

William H. Willimon
Resident Bishop Birmingham Area
The United Methodist Church

CHAPTER ONE

THE PREACHED WORD IS THE WORD OF GOD

"I will pour out my spirit on all flesh;
your sons and your daughters shall prophesy,
* your old men shall dream dreams,*
* and your young men shall see visions." (Joel 2:28 RSV)*

John Wesley, father of Methodism, ignited a revival that swept across the world. A major aspect of that revival was Wesley's preaching. He preached sometimes in open fields, sometimes in little Wesleyan chapels where the common folk of eighteenth-century England heard him gladly. Early on in his movement he published a book of his sermons that were transcribed by faithful followers and edited for publication. He insisted that his lay preachers read, inculcate, and imitate his *Sermons* before they attempted to preach on their own. In fact, Wesley's *Sermons* comprise an essential part of Methodist doctrine to this day.

And yet for most of us, reading Wesley's *Sermons* is an unedifying activity. (I have had the same disappointing experience in reading the sermons of Luther or Calvin.) The language sounds stilted and dry. The sermons are overly formal, devoid of illustrations and connections with everyday life, or any of those characteristics that we think are essential for sermons today. Of course they are not Wesley's sermons as they were actually preached. These are transcriptions for publication. Something was no doubt lost in the move from oral to written form. Still, one is baffled that thousands heard Wesley with such gratitude and to so strong an effect.

Perhaps Wesley the preacher possessed an impressive presence in the pulpit. A stirring voice and imposing stature command the respect of an audience. Wesley must have been a strong figure when he preached.

Well, forget it. Wesley had a tiny physique, even for his day. He stood about five feet two and had delicate features. His voice, while said to be pleasing, was rather frail. What was there about the man that made his sermons rend the hearts of his hearers? A Swedish visitor came all the way to England to hear him preach in 1769 and, after hearing him declared, "He has no great oratorical gifts, no outward appearance."[1]

What did Wesley have that made his sermons so powerful? The answer is *nothing*. It was not the man who made the message move people with such power, nor even the message itself, though Wesley's sermons are well crafted and theologically substantive. Wesley's sermons "worked," they taught, they moved, and they delighted (three characteristics that Augustine demanded of good sermons) because of God's speaking rather than Wesley's.

The reasons for any sermon speaking to the hearts, minds, and souls of the hearers are always more theological than anthropological, due more to the nature of God than the nature of the preacher or the hearers. "Theology" means literally "God words" (*theos* = God; *logoi* = words). But theology does not just mean words *about* God, our talk about the meaning of God. Theology also means God's talk, God's talk about the meaning of God to us. Christianity is a "revealed religion," which means that it is based upon the conviction and the experience of a loquacious God. Preaching is not merely what we say, even what John Wesley said, or what we hear, even the most astute of us listeners. Preaching is what God says.

Wesley's sermons spoke to people because the God of Israel and the church deemed it right to speak to people through Wesley's sermons. I cannot capture or completely reproduce the sound of the divine voice, or its effects, in my reading of Wesley's sermons, not because Wesley is of the eighteenth century and I am of the twenty-first but because preaching is something that God does rather than something that either I do or John Wesley does. We preach because God speaks, and a primary way for this God to speak is through preaching.

We preachers are subservient to the power of God to speak. As Paul put it in 1 Corinthians 3:7, "So neither the one who plants nor the one who waters is anything, but only God who gives the growth." We preachers, when compared with the mass of public speakers of various stripes, are distinguished by the rather unique quality that we do not work alone.

If you have never had your soul seized by God in a sermon, if you have never been surprised that through the frail, inadequate, poorly delivered, not fully comprehensible words of an ordinary woman or man preaching your life was changed, if you have never been swept away by the rush of divine revelation coming to you in a homily, then you may think that this talk about God speaking in preaching sounds silly.

Yet for the multitudes, which no one can number—who have been enlisted in God's great movement to take back the world, all those who heard their name called by God through a preacher, all those who risked life itself on the basis of nothing more than words heard in a sermon, the saints who have gone before us and who even now stand among us—the preached word has been, still is, the very Word of God.

I'm saying that God in Christ became incarnate in John Wesley's sermons. The Almighty God, who hung the stars and flung the planets in their courses, came close to humanity in preaching. The evidence for that outrageous claim is not in Wesley's sermons. The evidence is in the people he produced through his preaching, or more accurately, in the undeniable work God did through a preacher named Wesley. Our God talks, and talks a great deal, mainly through preaching.

Creation through Words

> In the beginning was the Word, and the Word was with God, and the Word was God. He was in the beginning with God. All things came into being through him, and without him not one thing came into being. (John 1:1-3)

Thus begins John's Gospel. In this majestic, poetic beginning we hear an echo of an earlier text, Genesis 1:1, "In the beginning when God created the heavens and the earth. . . ." There are gods who create worlds by having sex with other gods, or through a primal, cosmic battle between good and evil, chaos and order. But this God creates through nothing but a word. All this God has to do is to say the word, "Light!" and there is light. "Animals!" and there is now something where before there was nothing but formless void.

On a cloudless night this God called Abram, a nomadic desert sheik, out of his tent and promised to make a great nation from this childless old man and his aged wife Sarai. Though the world considered the old couple to be "barren," God promised Abram that his descendants would be as numerous as the stars and would comprise a nation that would be a "blessing to all the nations" (from Genesis 18). And all this would be on the basis of nothing more than a promise, nothing more than words. That's the way this God works.

When that promised people became numerous, they found themselves as slaves in Egypt, under the heel of the most powerful empire in the world. Moses is out in Midian, watching over his father-in-law's sheep. (Moses had killed a man back in Egypt and was hiding out in Midian.) Before an astounded Moses, a bush bursts into flame but is not consumed. Even more astounding, the bush speaks! (Exodus 3)

> "I am the Lord your God.
> "Now you go to the Pharaoh and say, let my people go."

Is that all? God is going to free the Hebrews on the basis of nothing but a command from a none-too-talented and untrained speaker like the murderer Moses? As Moses wants to know, "Who am I that I should go to the Pharaoh and say. . .?"

But that is the way this God works, creating something out of nothing, a people out of nobodies, free women and men out of slaves, all on the basis of nothing but words.

Those people, now free, are given a land "flowing with milk and honey," just as God had so sovereignly promised. But they wandered. They consorted with other gods, forgot their origins, forgot the God who had liberated and blessed them. So God sent a peculiar set of preachers called "prophets." These God-obsessed individuals were personally chosen by God to give the people of Israel the bad news of their coming exile, then to sustain them through the horrors of their Babylonian captivity, then to announce that they were going home, then to direct how they would reconstruct themselves as God's people—all on the basis of nothing but words. The prophets of Israel were poets who were preachers, preachers who were poets. They deconstructed old worlds and envisioned new worlds, with some of the pushiest, poetic, figurative, and powerful speech ever uttered, all on the basis of nothing but words.

In a 1551 sermon series on the prophet Micah, reformer John Calvin said that the whole purpose of the church is to preach. The reign of Christ is established, not by swords, says Calvin, but by the preaching of the Word. Calvin bases this assertion on the words of the prophet:

> And they shall beat their swords into plowshares,
>   and their spears into pruning hooks;
> nation shall not lift up sword against nation,
>   neither shall they learn war any more;
> but they shall sit every man under his vine and under his
>   fig tree,
>   and none shall make them afraid;
>   for the mouth of the LORD of hosts has spoken.
>   (Micah 4:3-4 RSV)

Peace on earth, swords transformed into plows, all on the basis of words from the "mouth of the LORD." As a contemporary commentator said of the preaching of Martin Luther, "By the power of his mouth hearts were melted like snow by the breath of spring as he showed the way to heaven's goods which had been closed for centuries."[2]

The Word of the Lord not only creates but also devastates. For something to be born, something must die; for there to be transformation, there must be dismantling. The Word of the Lord destroys what has been so that something new may come.

In the Bible, word precedes world. There is nothing until there are words to create something. The names are not necessarily connected to the thing but rather arise from the one who does the naming. Reality is linguistically constructed. Word precedes world. Words do not arise from things, but rather things are evoked by the Word. Word precedes all things. God said, "Let there be light." And there was. Yahweh allowed the earthling, Adam, to enjoy a bit of divine creativity by naming some of the cattle and birds (Genesis 2:20). Creativity is a word-derived phenomenon.

The New Testament opens with John the Baptist standing in the Jordan, calling people to get washed. John tells those who take comfort in the old order, "God can raise up a people out of the stones in this river if God must" (Matthew 3:9 author paraphrase).

God had done this before. From out of formless void, the *tohu wabohu,* God had spoken and there was life and light. On a starlit night, God called Abraham out of his tent, promising to make a great nation to bless the world from a man and woman as good as dead. And all this newness was created by nothing but words. Word makes world.

And then there came One among us, born as we are born, who was named Emmanuel, God with us, Word Made Flesh. And what did he do? He came preaching (Matthew 4:17). Luke records his first great assault upon the world-as-it-is was in a synagogue, in a pulpit, quoting his favorite prophet, " 'The Spirit of the Lord is upon me . . . to bring good news. . . .' " (Luke 4:18).

The Word Made Flesh was the embodied, active Word, healing the sick, embracing the untouchable, enlightening the blind, turning over the temple tables, and riding into Jerusalem in triumph. But mostly he spoke. He assaulted the world, not with violent deeds but with a barrage of words—parables that shocked, evoked, amused, and disclosed; sermons that often ended with a riot; blessings, curses, proverbs, and prophesies. He said he brought a new kingdom and some—not that many, not many of the wise and powerful, but enough to attract the worried attention of the authorities—hailed him as "King." He sure talked often enough of his present and coming "Kingdom of God," but that was about all he did to inaugurate his reign. He just talked.

His talk was enough to get him tried, tortured, and horribly, publicly, humiliatingly executed. His metaphors were sometimes obscure, his parables hard to follow, and his meaning elusive, but he spoke clearly enough for the governmental and religious authorities to get his point. They crucified him in their attempt to get him quiet.

For three days the silence was deafening.

The accounts of what happened on the third day after his crucifixion, the first day of the week, are diverse and confusing, as if the witnesses did not know how to bring what they had seen and heard to speech. Some women (where were the men?) who loved him came to his tomb in the early morning darkness and in grief, and there they were met by an angel. "'Why do you seek the living among the dead?'" the angel impudently asked them (Luke 24:5 RSV). "He has risen, he is not here. . . . he is going before you to Galilee" (Mark 16:6-7 RSV).

And the startled women race all the way back to the male disciples and announce, "He is risen!" They thus became the first witnesses to the resurrection, the first evangelists to spread the good news, "He is loose! The story is not over; it is just beginning!"

Why Galilee? It is an undistinguished location by any account. Why, on the first day after his resurrection, did he go there? Galilee is where his preaching began. He has gone back home, back to the hinterland where his movement began, to resume his preaching, this time as resurrected Christ.

Luke says that while a couple of the disciples were walking that very afternoon from Jerusalem to a little village of Emmaus, a stranger appeared and walked with them. The stranger "opened the scriptures to them," revealing all that the prophets had said (Luke 24). That evening, seated around the dinner table, when the stranger took the bread and broke it and gave it, they saw. The stranger vanished, and they ran all the way back to Jerusalem shouting, "The women were right! He has appeared to us!"

John says that very evening the disciples were gathered "behind locked doors for fear." They had good reason to fear, having witnessed what the authorities did to Jesus. And now that they were alone, and Jesus dead, with they themselves as his betrayers, fear is what they felt (John 20).

John says that the risen Christ stood among them and said, "Peace." He spoke to them. He offered them his risen body as validation of his resurrection. He gave them power to forgive sins, and then he vanished.

Why would the risen Christ appear first to these fearful ordinary men and women, his disciples, who had demonstrated so conclusively their failure to follow him and be his courageous disciples? Why would the risen Christ not appear to some powerful, influential, public figure like Pilate or Augustus?

He came to the ones who had fled the conversation once the going got rough. He came to the very ones who had so disappointed and forsaken him, those whom he had so patiently taught and yet who had so patently misunderstood his every word. He came to them and said, in effect, "Let's talk. As I was saying. . . ."

And thus was the church born, and thus were we all made witnesses of resurrection and preachers of good news. The sermons are not over. They are just beginning.

And the conversation was resumed. Time and again in our history with the God of the church and Israel, when we have betrayed the love of God with our infidelity, when we have misunderstood, when we have fled into the darkness or stopped up our ears and hardened our hearts, this God has returned to us and has resumed the conversation. Thus Paul prayed that God might "open to us a door for the word" (Colossians 4:3), acknowledging that the means of this conversation are at God's initiative, not ours.

In that divine-human dialogue, in that conversation, this God has proved to be remarkably resourceful and imaginative, full of stratagems and devices—the Incarnation, Word Made Flesh, being the most imaginative of all. There is a relentlessness about the speech of this God, an effusive loquaciousness, a dogged determination not to rest, not to fall silent, not to cease striving until every single one of us is part of the conversation.

Therein is our hope. Here is a divine-human dialogue that is initiated and, at every turn in the road sustained, by a living, resourceful, long-winded God, thank God.

If God should stop talking, if God should withdraw, even for a moment, into apophatic, empty silence, then the mountains would fall, chaos would overwhelm, the light would become darkness, and death would have the last word. Yet God's creative, life-giving, people-forming, intrusive Word keeps creating, keeps being made flesh, keeps pushing in, keeps having the last say.

The prophet Isaiah hears a divine promise related to the divine word:

> "So shall my word be that goes forth from my mouth;
>   it shall not return to me empty,
> but it shall accomplish that which I purpose,
>   and prosper in the thing for which I sent it."
>   (Isaiah 55:11 RSV)

This is the only basis for Christian preaching; its only hope. This is the good news. So when Paul's preaching authority was challenged by some in Galatia, Paul mounted no other defense for himself than this:

> For I would have you know, brethren, that the gospel which was preached by me is not man's gospel. For I did not receive it from man, nor was I taught it, but it came through a revelation of Jesus Christ. (Galatians 1:11-12 RSV)

To be sure, Paul is defending himself as an apostle, but Paul's defense is that which applies to every preacher of the gospel. The preacher's authority and authorization rest not upon an orthodox, faithful reiteration of church tradition, not upon the ecclesiastical confirmation by officials of the church. It is "through a revelation of Jesus Christ." It is a bold, audacious claim, a claim that could lead the clamant to self-delusion. Yet it is the scandalous affirmation of faith upon which preaching rests.

On the basis of this story, as well as their own experience, the Protestant Reformers were able to link our speaking in preaching with God's own discourse. In a sermon on 1 Samuel, John Calvin dared to speak of contemporary pastors as prophets, like Samuel, who are "the very mouth of God." As Bullinger asserts in the Second Helvetic Confession, "The preaching of the word of God *is* the Word of God." This is an astounding claim to make for the speaking of mere mortals like us preachers and for the hearing of mere mortals like our congregations. Yet it is a no more astounding claim than that made by Jesus: "Whoever listens to you listens to me" (Luke 10:16). It is a claim that rests upon faith in a gracious God who condescends to us mere mortals through preaching. It is faith that is born of the story that begins with, "And God said. . . ."

CHAPTER TWO

THE PROPHETIC WORD

> The voice of the LORD is powerful;
>   the voice of the LORD is full of majesty.
> The voice of the LORD breaks the cedars;
>   the LORD breaks the cedars of Lebanon. . . .
> The voice of the LORD causes the oaks to whirl,
>   and strips the forest bare;
>   and in his temple all say, "Glory!" . . .
> May the LORD bless his people with peace!
> (Psalm 29:4-5, 9, 11)

In his Yale Lectures on Preaching in 1877, Phillips Brooks, the eloquent Boston preacher, gave American preaching its most durable definition. Preaching is "truth through personality." Brooks spent more of his lecture on the second half of the equation, the personality of the preacher, than on the first, the truth of preaching.

> Truth through personality is our description of real preaching. The truth must come really through the person, not merely over his lips, . . . through his character, his affections, his whole intellectual and moral being.[1]

Brooks's definition of preaching stresses at least part of the nature of incarnational truth. Here is truth that must be embodied in order to be received. The definition is not only congruent with an incarnational faith in the Word Made Flesh, it also fit nicely in the burgeoning science of psychology and personality development in late-nineteenth-century America. Brooks's characterization of preaching was congruent with William James's philosophy-as-psychology that was to capture the American intellectual imagination. Today, when asked, "What do you want in a preacher?" most congregations of my acquaintance will say, "A warm personality," or "A real and genuine person," before they say, "Biblical fidelity," or "Theological substance."

Brooks tended to stress the personality of the preacher more than the nature of the truth communicated through the personality. And so do most contemporary homileticians. Modern Americans live in what one commentator has described as "The Psychological Society" in which psychological problems are the only problems that concern us. "It's all inside," is the advertising slogan of one of our department stores. Modernity has a way of detaching us from the world and pushing us ever deeper into ourselves. We tend to think of the world as internal before it becomes external. We think that we think inside out. We have these innate ideas, these stirrings within us, and preaching evokes and provokes them, projects them out upon the world, and this we call "reality." It's all inside.

The Roman orator Quintillian defined a good speech as "a good person speaking well." The character of the speaker is vitally important for the audience's reception of the speech. Thus Brooks stood in an ancient tradition in characterizing preaching as "truth through personality." Today I do not hear that much discussion about the character and personality of the preacher, but I do hear a great deal of talk about the personality of the congregation, truth communicated through a personality to a group of personalities. The modern congregation's "felt needs," modern prejudices, limitations, and possibilities are the major concerns of contemporary homiletical thought.

It is my judgment that current preaching is in great need of theological refurbishment. We desperately need something from the outside. We must recover a sense of preaching as something that God does—a theological matter before it is an anthropological matter—preaching as the business of God before it is our business. In other words, if Brooks were lecturing at Yale on preaching today, I hope that he would expend most of his effort on truth—specifically, the One who is "the way, the truth, and the life"—rather than on the preacher's personality.

The personality of the preacher is noteworthy mainly as the person of someone who has seen and heard something, a messenger who has been grasped by a message, someone who has been addressed. Otherwise, in my experience, the personalities of us preachers are not that interesting. Good preaching, said theologian Karl Barth, is like a person standing on a street corner pointing upward into the sky. Of course a crowd gathers, everyone craning the neck upward, attempting to see whatever it is that the person who is pointing upward sees. Theology reminds us preachers that the crucial matter is not so much that we eloquently point upward but rather that we see something that merits drawing a crowd.

Preaching, to be truly Christian preaching, must be reflexive, responsive. Something has happened to us and to our world, therefore we speak about it. Martin Luther characterized the gospel as the *verbum externum*, the "external word," a word that is not self-derived, a word that comes to us from outside our personal experiences or interior ruminations. Perhaps this is why "faith comes from hearing." The gospel, which gives rise to faith, comes to us from the outside. It must be spoken to us, told to us rather than arising out of us. Preaching, in this Lutheran characterization, is truth assaulting, forming, reforming personalities, rather than truth merely being expressed through a passive person.

In 1537 Luther began a series of sermons on the Gospel of John. It is clear that Luther undertook this task not because he wanted to get something off his chest, not because he had something welling up from within him that he wanted to say, but rather because he had been confronted with a Word that lay outside his world, a Word that created in him and his hearers a new world. He came to the Gospel of John as one might be met by a stranger. The stranger must be encountered in all of his strangeness, in his sheer otherness, and allowed to have his say, or one has not really met the stranger. This Luther did with the Fourth Gospel.

Luther said that the preacher who would introduce so strange a gospel as the Gospel of John to a congregation must first immerse himself in the peculiar way that the Bible talks and then cultivate the courage to say what has been heard, regardless of the reactions of the hearers. The preacher

> must remain conversant with this evangelist; to this end we must familiarize ourselves with his way of speaking. Therefore we propose to consider his Gospel in the name of the Lord, discuss it, and preach it as long as we are able, to the glory of our Lord Christ and to our own welfare, comfort, and salvation, without worrying whether the world shows much interest in it. Nonetheless, there will always be a few who will hear God's precious Word with delight; and for their sakes, too, we must preach it. For since God provides people whom He orders to preach, He will surely also supply and send listeners who will take this instruction to heart.[2]

Note how different this statement is than the approach of contemporary homiletics. We tend to think that the test of a sermon is the impact upon the listeners. Have they heard what is said? Do they consent to the argument? Are they emotionally moved? Have their lives been enriched?

Luther says that the challenge is not in the listeners but in the Gospel. We are to preach not for the hearers but "to the glory of our Lord Christ . . . without worrying whether the world shows much interest in it." We are to love the text more than we love our congregational context. We preachers are to worry more about what is being said and how well we can replicate that word than we are to worry about whether or not what is being said in the Gospel is being heard in the world. Thus in a sermon on Matthew, Luther said that the test of our ministry as preachers is "not whether many or few people believe or do not believe, are damned or saved" but rather "fidelity to the Word of God."[3]

In a world of "Seeker Services," and "User Friendly" churches, I submit that Luther's view of preaching is countercultural as well as counterecclesial in the extreme. Before preaching can be communication, exhortation, admonition, comfort, or motivation, it must be prayerful listening for the Word of God. Preaching can be said to be "effective" only because it is true. It is not through psychology, sociology, or skillful rhetoric that we reach people but rather through theology—*and God said.* Without hearing that Word, preaching has nothing to say. Otherwise preaching is but a blasphemous attempt to speak in the place of God rather than to speak for God. Thus prayer is the first step in sermon preparation, and all subsequent steps of biblical study, sermon construction, and even sermon delivery are aspects of prayer. Prayer is listening to God more than prayer is talking to God. The humility, the admission of emptiness and need, and the expectant attentiveness that are the disciplines of prayer are also the disciplines of sermon preparation. Preachers are to say what they have heard, whether the congregation hears or refuses to hear.

Nevertheless, Luther is not pessimistic about the fruitfulness of the undertaking, even when the preacher tackles so great an assignment as preaching through the Gospel of John because the same commanding God who graciously "provides people whom He orders to preach" will likewise graciously "also supply and send listeners who will take this instruction to heart." In other words, not only is the substance the "truth" of preaching God's responsibility but also the hearers as well. Here is "truth" not as some abstract ideal or concept but rather truth as a speaking subject, truth as a person who speaks, truth as none other than Jesus Christ himself.

Luther's Augustinian theology depicts preaching as the action of the unmerited grace of God. We are beggars, we preachers and we hearers, needing a God to give us that which we cannot have by our own efforts. Our faith in preaching is not based upon preaching's effectiveness but rather upon its truth, a truth that graciously reaches out to us and gives us what we need to hear as the way, the truth, and the life. Take Jesus' parable of the seed as a theological account of preaching. Although there is much waste in preaching, many words that don't take root, there is also rather miraculous harvest. The Word has in itself the power, given by God, to effect that which it proclaims. The Word germinates, springs to life, grows, overcomes all obstacles. Despite the soil, weeds, and all the other obstacles, the seed gives a rich, miraculous harvest (Matthew 13:18-33).

Next Sunday, if once again my congregation appears to be unmoved and unimpressed by my homiletical efforts, I intend to ascribe their lack of response to God! Our job as preachers is to stand up and speak the truth as God gives it to us; congregational response is God's business.

The toughest assignment for us preachers is the continual cultivation of a respect for and a love of the otherness, the strangeness, and the ever supple liveliness of the truth that is Jesus Christ. The next toughest assignment is constant prayer for the gift of the guts to speak that truth when it is given to us, just like Luther said.

In this cultivation, we contemporary preachers are heirs to the great prophetic tradition of Israel and the church. Prophets in the Bible are not those who peer into the future and predict events that other people don't see (which is how they are mischaracterized by some in evangelical Christianity and pop culture). Nor are prophets carping social critics a bit to the left of the Democratic Party (as they are misconstrued by some in liberal Christianity). Prophets are those who have been assaulted by, and are now obsessed with, the truth of God. Prophets are those who have unusual gifts for discernment into the purposes of God and who are unusually bold in bringing those purposes to speech.

You will note that in biblical accounts of the origins of prophets like Amos, Isaiah, or Jeremiah—some of Israel's greatest prophets—we have almost nothing about their families, their places of origin, or prior development before they were called by God to be speakers of the truth. Matters of family, personality, origin, and prior development are irrelevant to prophets. (Note that we know almost nothing of Jesus from birth to age thirty.) The only thing that matters is, "The word of the Lord came to me and said. . . ." Prophets are created out of nothing by the vocation of a God who summons some people to speak God's truth. The prophets never claim to be astute political analysts, insightful students of the human condition, or wise sages. They claim that their words are God's words. They risk everything to speak because they are confident that God has spoken to them. Whereas the prophets put God's words into written form, current Christian preachers put the prophets' written words of God into oral, proclaimed form. When it comes to the significance of prophets or preachers, the main thing is the Word of God.

Consider the call of Jeremiah in the book of Jeremiah, chapter one. It is as if before God's call, there is no Jeremiah. When called, Jeremiah protests that he is "only a youth," that he has no theological or rhetorical training or gifts. But God replies with the commanding "go," and "tell." It is the divinely empowering, vocational truth that matters, not the personality of the prophet. In other words, reading Jeremiah 1 is something akin theologically to reading Genesis 1. Creation *ex nihilo*.

Prophets, speakers of the truth, begin in the heart of God, in God's relentless determination to have a people, a family. Through this family, God intends to bless all the world's families. And how does this God get what God wants? Through words. Rarely are divine words directly spoken. Most of the time they require an intermediary, some human being to speak for God. This God rarely works solo. Rather, this God tends to summon and enlist ordinary women and men to speak for God. Those who are thus summoned are called prophets.

While Augustine was preaching in Hippo in the fall of 395, he became aware that the Christians of the city were reveling in the feast of Laetitia, often coming to church in a drunk and disorderly manner. "By the hidden foreordination of the Almighty God," said Augustine, the assigned Gospel was from Matthew 7:6, Jesus' warning not to cast pearls before swine or what is holy to dogs. Augustine saw the text as a divine summons to chastise his congregation for their lingering paganism: "I discoursed therefore concerning dogs and swine in such a way as to compel those who clamour with obstinate barking against the divine precepts, and who are given up to the abominations of carnal pleasures, to blush for shame."[4] Though the record does not show how his congregation responded to their preacher's calling them dogs and pigs, it was for Augustine a good example of the way in which ordinary fidelity to the Word enables us to speak the right word in due season in a prophetic, truthful way, giving us something to say that we in no wise could have had on our own. By being more securely attached to the Scriptures, by listening to God before we want to be heard by our congregations, we become the prophetic pastors God calls us to be.

> Then I heard the voice of the Lord saying, "Whom shall I send, and who will go for us?" And I said, "Here am I; send me!" And he said, "Go and say to this people. . . ." (Isaiah 6:8-9)

Prophets All

A little tattle-tale comes running to father Moses, "Daddy Moses, Eldad and Medad are prophesying in the camp" (see Numbers 11:26-27).[5] Earlier the Lord, after speaking to Moses, took a notion to spread a little Spirit on some of the elders, Spirit which the Lord had previously disbursed mainly to Moses. Now, having received the gift of the Spirit, Eldad and Medad get down-right loquacious, and begin speaking up for God. Joshua, one of the "chosen men" doesn't like this effusive spirit. "My lord Moses, stop them!" (11:28).

We can't have ordinary, uncredentialed, uncertified people prophesying, speaking for God. Today Medad and Eldad, tomorrow my son or daughter. Joshua asks Moses for a prophetic restraining order.

Moses' response was, "Would that all the LORD's people were prophets, and that the LORD would put his spirit on them!" (Numbers 11:29).

Moses, who himself had been none too adept at speaking the truth to the powers that be until God gave him a spirited shove (see Exodus 3–4), is not miserly of spirit. Would to God that all of God's people were prophets! There are never too many spirit-gifted prophets.

The Common Lectionary on Pentecost wisely uses this obscure episode from Numbers 11 as a setup for an even more effusive, more prophetic spiritual breakout in Acts 2. At Pentecost, we were all gathered in one place. Then there was a rush of wind, tongues of fire, Holy Spirit. And everyone began to speak, "telling in our own tongues the mighty works of God" (Acts 2:11 RSV). As in Numbers 11, the Spirit's gift is the gift of speech, prophecy. As in Numbers 11, the Spirit's creation of a multitude of preachers results in communal bewilderment (Acts 2:6). Amazed and astonished, we ask "What does this mean?"

In reply to the mocking of the mob, Peter speaks. Only a short time before, we left Peter with the maid in a courtyard (Luke 22:54ff.). Peter could find nothing to say when she accused, "You also were with the Galilean." Now Peter is the spokesperson for the church, the major interpreter of the miracle of Pentecost. Apparently, Pentecost has enabled Peter to find his tongue. Peter explains the ruckus in the upper room by reference to the prophet Joel. In earlier days, the Spirit was poured out on a few gifted (or at the least, offensive) individuals called prophets. But there will be a day, according to Joel 2:28-32, when God's Spirit shall be poured out on all. All. Even among the typically voiceless—old women and old men (pensioners, usually institutionalized, non-productive therefore not valued), young people out of work, underpaid maids, janitors—God's Spirit shall descend in the later days, bringing things to speech. Those who never appear on the pages of *The New York Times*, those who were never asked to say a few words at the microphone, shall speak.

Later the world would marvel that such "uneducated, common" people like Peter (Acts 4:13 RSV) were speaking, each telling in their own words "God's deeds of power" (Acts 2:11). The holy wind at Pentecost is power unto speech. The gift of Acts 2 is the gift of prophecy. That day, surely somebody remembered Moses' swaggering, "Would that *all* of God's people were prophets!" That day is now; those prophets are us. When we are baptized, we are baptized into the ministry of preaching the truth. By virtue of baptism, we're all prophets now.

And what makes a person a prophet is not the possession of unusual courage or insight (many of the Old Testament prophets have neither) but rather the prophet's subservience to the truth. Not long ago, a person emerged from my place of preaching quite upset by the sermon. As I stood there, listening to her complaint, I thought, "I don't really care that you were upset by the sermon." My lack of concern for her disapproval is amazing considering that I am a coward by nature. (I was elected president of my school class every year from the time I was twelve. One does not get elected to office by being truthful.) And yet here, at the door of a church, I was standing, amazingly impervious to the assaults of an offended church member. Simply by going about the tasks of preaching, teaching, showing up on a Sunday, attempting to listen to the word, trying to bring the truth to speech, I had been made into something of a prophet. My personality had been greatly enhanced by the power of the truth.

The purpose of my preaching, the test for a "good" sermon, is its ability to be enlisted by God as part of God's prophet-making process. God intends to have a people who speak the truth, who testify to the world of God's great, loving assault upon the world. As Moses put it, "Would that all the LORD's people were prophets, and that the LORD would put his spirit on them!"

In Acts 2, the pentecostal test for prophecy is not how outrageous we preachers have managed to be in the pulpit but rather how many people we have produced who are able to say, No: people who can speak the truth to power, people who can go up and stand before the Pharaoh and impudently tell him that he is not fully in charge of the world—old men and women, janitors and maids with visions and dreams and who don't mind telling the world about them.

From my reading of Acts 2 and Luke's account of the birth of the church, I derive a few principles for prophecy: (1) The Spirit has given the world a *prophetic community*, not simply a few outspoken social critics; (2) The goal of the Spirit's descent is the creation of a *polis*, a people who look, speak, and act differently from the world's notions of community; and (3) No individual prophets are possible without the existence of a peculiar prophetic community whose life together is vibrant enough to produce a band of prophets who do not mind telling the truth to one another and the world, no matter what. The goal of our pastoral care, preaching, visitation, prayer, and praise is the production of a whole gaggle of prophets who will let God use them to get back what God owns.

The prophetic community is composed of young and old, maids and janitors, sons and daughters, those who have not had much opportunity in the world's scheme of things to speak. In other words, *The Holy Spirit produces uppity speech.* When once I asked an African American friend of mine, "Why does African American preaching tend to get loud and raucous?" he replied, "Because my people have been told so often, for so long, that we ought to be seen and not heard, or better, invisible and quiet. We are to stand politely on the margins while the majority culture does its thing. So the church gathers my people and enables them to strut and shout, to find their voice, to stand up and be heard."

Much Christian worship ought to be predicated on the premise that, if we can get a group of ordinary, otherwise voiceless people to strut their stuff before the throne of God on Sunday, we will be able to do the same before the city council, or the Pentagon, or the administration on Monday. The Acts of the Apostles is in great part the story of how a bunch of "uneducated, common" people (Acts 4:13 RSV), with the empowerment of the Holy Spirit, got too big for their britches and by the power of the Risen Christ "[turned] the world upside down" (Acts 17:6).

Fortunately, when these prophets speak out and speak up, they do not have to come up with something to say on their own. Jesus promises that the Holy Spirit will give them the right words.

> When they bring you before the synagogues and the rulers and the authorities, do not be anxious how or what you are to answer or what you are to say; for the Holy Spirit will teach you in that very hour what you ought to say. (Luke 12:11-12 RSV)

In preparation for a Sunday one fall, I checked the Lectionary and, to my dismay, the first lesson is assigned from the book of Proverbs. Generally, I dislike the book of Proverbs with its lack of theological content, its long lists of platitudinous advice, its "Do this. . . ." and "Don't do that. . . . " Pick up your socks. Be nice to salesclerks. It doesn't hurt to be nice. Proverbs is something like being trapped on a long road trip with your mother, or at least William Bennett.

Still, I stuck with the text, Proverbs 22:1, "A good name is to be chosen rather than great riches . . . " (RSV).

I told the congregation that Proverbs tends to be full of conventional, worldly wisdom, tips for better living, helpful hints for making it through life. Here is literature of the establishment, words that the old pass on to the young to keep the kids on the straight and narrow.

But this particular proverb, 22:1, may challenge that. "A good name is to be chosen rather than great riches." A value judgment is being made. One way is "better than" another. Do we believe it? How many of us are here at the university to get a good name? Donald Trump believes the proverb that says, "Go for the gold!" Put this on a T-shirt and wear this about campus for a couple of weeks and let me know how you fare in fraternity rush, "A GOOD NAME IS TO BE CHOSEN RATHER THAN GREAT RICHES." We live in a society where there is not much that we are unwilling to sacrifice, even our reputation, in order to get the gold.

Since the sermon was from the book of Proverbs—conventional wisdom of the establishment—I was more than surprised when, at the end of the service, a sophomore emerged from the chapel saying, "That was a great sermon. Thanks. I now know that I'm not going to law school, and tonight I'm going to call my old man and tell him that he can go to hell."

"Well, don't mention where you were this morning at eleven when you call him," said I.

Even seemingly tame, timid words of conventional wisdom can, once the Holy Spirit gets hold of them, be dynamite if the preacher will trust the peculiar truth that is the gospel and trust the Holy Spirit to make a true and lively word for us today.

The pastor as prophet is the one who keeps reminding the church of how oddly wonderful it is that God has chosen ordinary folk like us to help take back the world, that God has chosen "what is foolish in the world to shame the wise, God chose what is weak in the world to shame the strong, God chose what is low and despised in the world, even things that are not, to bring to nothing things that are" (1 Corinthians 1:27-28 RSV).

Therefore our prophetic preaching has as its goal the evocation of prophetic schoolteachers, shopkeepers, nursing home residents, and sixteen-year-olds who can speak the truth to power. Not everyone is called to be a preacher to the congregation. As Ephesians 4 says, "The gifts he gave were that some would be apostles, some prophets, some evangelists, some pastors and teachers" (v. 11). What is the chief purpose of all these divinely bestowed gifts? "To equip the saints for the work of ministry, for building up the body of Christ" (v. 12). Paul is not talking about an established order of clergy but rather the way that God gives baptismal gifts to all for the edification of the church. Ordained clergy preach to the church so that the church might preach to the world.

First Peter is speaking to all Christians, all the baptized, not just the church's leaders or clergy in saying,

> But you are a chosen race, a royal priesthood, a holy nation, God's own people, that you may declare the wonderful deeds of him who called you out of darkness into his marvelous light. (1 Peter 2:9 RSV)

Luther says that all Christians, by virtue of their baptism, are called to declare the wonderful deeds of God, to preach. Yet not all are called publicly to preach to the church. "Although we are all equally priests, we cannot all publicly minister and teach. We ought not to do so even if we could."[6] Husbands are to preach to wives; wives are to preach to husbands; parents are to preach to children; all of us are called to preach to the world. But because we can't all preach at the same time when the church gathers, the church selects some to preach to the church on Sunday so that the whole church can join Jesus in preaching to the rest of the world all week long. Those selected are called pastors, preachers, servants of the word.

The real test of preaching that is done by an ordained pastor is not the praise of the public, nor even its faithfulness to the original Greek of the biblical text, but rather the ability of the pastor's sermon to evoke a prophetic people.

Ephesians 4:15-16 establishes a link between truth-telling and community, between truth-telling and maturity:

> But speaking the truth in love, we must grow up in every way into him who is the head, into Christ, from whom the whole body, joined and knit together by every ligament with which it is equipped, as each part is working properly, promotes the body's growth in building itself up in love.

"Speaking the truth in love" is linked to maturity and growth. Without truthful speech, we are left with immature Christians. In the church, in my experience, we usually opt for love at the expense of truth. Of course, from a gospel point of view, dishonest love is hardly love at all. On the basis of Ephesians 4:15-16, prophetic speech is an aspect of the practice of love, a necessary component of Christian unity among a people for whom there is "one Lord, one faith, one baptism, one God and Father of all" (Ephesians 4:5-6). Too often, in too many congregations, unity is purchased by the world's means—suppression of information, deceitful flattery, niceness, and subterfuge—rather than through the Christ-appointed means of speaking the truth in love. In order to have unity or love worthy of the designation "Christian," we need to be more in love with truth than with either unity or love.

A woman accosted me at the front door, at the end of service, after I had preached on forgiveness.

"Do you mean to tell me that Jesus expects me to forgive my abusive husband who made my life hell for ten years until I got the courage to leave him. . . . I'm supposed to forgive him?"

I got nervous. Defensively I said, "Well, we only have twenty minutes for the sermon. I can't properly qualify and nuance everything. But I do feel that, though I am deeply concerned about the problem of spouse abuse, I do feel that Jesus does tell us to forgive our enemies, and who is a greater enemy than your ex-husband? I do think that Jesus probably did mean for us to. . . ."

"Good!" she said. "Just checking!" With that she went forth, going forth, I think, with a burden placed upon her back, a burden not of her own devising, to walk a narrow way quite different from the ways of the world. Who told me as a preacher to attempt to lessen that gap, that life-giving gospel gap, between her and the gospel? Who told me that she was unable to be called by Jesus? Why did I think that she could not be a prophet?

As that eloquent English preacher of a century ago, P. T. Forsyth, said:

> The one great preacher in history, . . . is the church. And the first business of the individual preacher is to enable the church to preach. Yet so that he is not its echo but its living voice, not the echo of its consciousness but the organ of its gospel. Either he gives the church utterance, or he gives it insight into the gospel it utters. He is to preach to the church from the gospel so that with the church he may preach the gospel to the world. He is so to preach to the church that he shall also preach *from* the church. That is to say, he must be a sacrament to the church, that with the church he may become a missionary to the world.[7]

CHAPTER THREE

THE BIBLICAL WORD

W hen the great theologian Karl Barth gave his lectures on preaching, under the gathering cloud of Nazism with thousands in the German church casting their lot with Hitler, Barth said that the only thing that could save the church now was strictly, exclusively, determinedly biblical preaching. But Barth also said that if there is one thing worse than being a nonbiblical preacher it was being a boring one. What is the remedy against boredom, that bane of homiletical existence? Barth said that the remedy was to be biblical:

> Preachers must not be boring. To a large extent the pastor and boredom are synonymous concepts. Listeners often think that they have heard already what is being said in the pulpit. They have long since known it themselves. The fault certainly does not lie with them alone. Against boredom the only defense is again being biblical. If a sermon is biblical, it will not be boring. Holy Scripture is in fact so interesting and has so much that is new and exciting to tell us that listeners cannot even think about dropping off to sleep.[1]

Preaching is prior to the New Testament. The Bible was spoken before it was written. The written, recorded, and remembered scriptural word is therefore subsequent to and derivative of the contemporaneous, preached word. All Scripture is, in its various forms, proclamation remembered, recollected, and reformed in literary form. We will read Scripture in a way that is faithful to its intentions if we read Scripture as a sort of sermon before we read it as history, mythology, literature, biology, or doctrine. Scripture may proclaim through literary modes that resemble what the world calls history, or literature, myth, or cosmology, but we do the Bible a disservice any time we read it without being cognizant of its essentially theological, homiletical intent.

On the other hand, today's preaching is derivative of yesterday's scriptural word. In preaching, the written word returns to its original form of the spoken word as Scripture again becomes proclamation. Preaching is that sort of public speaking that strives never to be original. Preaching is Christian only when it is biblical, when it is obviously derivative of, submissive to, and controlled by the biblical word. Therefore the most important disciplines required of a preacher tend to be those disciplines associated with the preacher's subservience to Scripture. No preacher speaks without having first prayerfully allowed Scripture to speak.

We have a sketch of a sermon given by Moses in Exodus 19. This is the sermonic prelude to the Decalogue, the Ten Commandments:

> And Moses went up to God, and the LORD called to him out of the mountain, saying, "Thus you shall say to the house of Jacob, and tell the people of Israel: You have seen what I did to the Egyptians, and how I bore you on eagles' wings and brought you to myself. Now therefore, if you will obey my voice and keep my covenant, you shall be my own possession among all peoples; for all the earth is mine, and you shall be to me a kingdom of priests and a holy nation. There are the words which you shall speak. . . ." (Exodus 19:3-6 RSV)

Note that Moses' sermon begins in remembrance, a virtual summary of Exodus 19–24. From memory ("You have seen . . .") the sermon moves toward exhortation ("Now therefore, if you will obey my voice . . ."). This is a typical biblical move, a typical homiletical move from recollection to performance, from memory of what God has done to statement of our present responsibility before God. Israel never tired of remembering the exodus as the basis for its life with God. The people of God exist as a creation of God, as a response to something that God has initiated. We look and live differently from other people because we recall our salvation, how we were created out of nothing by a God who "bore you on eagles' wings and brought you to myself."

Thus Scripture is not merely a helpful resource for preaching, it is the genesis of preaching, the rationale for preaching, the substance and the means of preaching. When we preach from the Scriptures, to the congregation, the Bible is living in its native habitat. It is functioning as it was intended. When the Bible is given over to scholars in some college department of religion who are subservient to the academy rather than to the church, it is often made to answer questions that are of little interest to the originating intentions of Scripture itself. Favorite historical-critical questions—*What is the earliest strata of this passage? How can this statement be credible to modern, scientific, western minds? Are these the genuine words of Jesus?*—are not as relevant as Scripture's originating, homiletical question: *Will you come forward, be part of a new, countercultural people of God, and follow Jesus where he leads you?*

Scripture speaks for itself, beyond our interpretation, sometimes despite our interpretation, through the enlivening, empowering of the Holy Spirit. The great Syrian preacher Ephrem (306–73) begins a poetic meditation on the book of Genesis by noting what happened to him when he turned toward the first verses of Genesis, only to find that this book, its lines and verses, were turning toward him:

> I read the opening of this book
> And I was filled with joy,
> For its verses and lines
> Spread out their arms to welcome me;
> The first rushed out and kissed me,
> And led me on to its companion;

And when I reached that verse
Wherein it is written
The story of Paradise,
It lifted me up and transported me
From the bosom of the book
To the very bosom of Paradise.[2]

Every preacher, in turning toward Scripture as a source for a sermon, is turning toward a living, speaking personality in documentary form that opens its arms toward us and rushes out to meet us in order to speak to us, through us, so that the church might be lifted up and transported to where God is.

Sometime during the mid-fifth century BC, Israel returned from exile.[3] Their beloved Jerusalem lay in ruins. A decision was made to rebuild the walls, a first step toward reclaiming Israel's identity as a people. During the reconstruction, a scroll was found, "the book of the law of Moses, which the LORD had given to Israel" (Nehemiah 8:1). Before the Water Gate, from morning until midday, in the presence of all the people, the priest Ezra read and "all the people were attentive to the book of the law" (8:3). Ezra stood upon a wooden platform and read. Ezra's fellow priests "gave the sense" of the words being read, "so that the people understood the reading" (8:8).

The people wept when they heard the words read and interpreted. They wept for joy at finally having recovered words lost to them in exile. They wept for sadness at how far they had strayed from God's appointed way.

Ezra told them not to weep. He proclaimed the day a great holiday, holy day, telling them to go and have a great party, "for the joy of the LORD is your strength" (8:10). They celebrated greatly because "they had understood the words that were declared to them" (8:12).

Here is a portrait of Israel at its best. Here is a snapshot of what would become Israel's tradition of the synagogue. The word is read and interpreted in worship; the people weep and then celebrate and align their lives accordingly. Israel is constituted, corrected, resurrected, and redeemed by words. As Walter

Brueggemann says in his commentary on Nehemiah 8, "This peculiar community is not self-generated, but understands itself in terms of a special authorization in a script available for steady and regular, attentive reiteration."[4] Christian clergy stand in that place once occupied by Ezra as public readers and interpreters of Scripture. Like Israel, the church is gathered, not as the world gathers on the basis of race, gender, nation, or class. These words of Scripture are not spoken merely in order to elicit agreement or noble feelings among the hearers but rather to form, reform, the hearers. It is the nature of Scripture to be "political," that is, formative. It is the nature of Scripture to want power over our lives. It is the nature of Scripture not so much to want to speak to our world but rather to absorb our world into the biblical world. So David H. Kelsey says that we come to the Bible not merely with the question, " 'What does the Bible say?' " but also, " 'What is God using the Bible to do to us?' "[5] In reading the Bible, God is not merely being revealed to us but is allowed to have God's way with us.

Our earliest detailed account of a Sunday service in the early church is that provided in Justin Martyr's *Apology* (c. 150):

> And on that day called Sunday, all who live in cities or in the country gather together to one place, and the memoirs of the apostles and the writings of the prophets are read, as long as time permits: then, when the reader has ceased, the president verbally instructs, and exhorts to the imitation of these good things.

Here we see all the elements of the Christian Service of the Word: the church gathers its scattered people, the church reads from Scripture and engages in acts of narration and remembrance, and then the church hears instruction and exhortation—that is, preaching—in order that Christians may embody what they have heard read and proclaimed.

As preachers, it is our peculiar service to the church, as its lead biblical interpreters, to lay the story of Israel and the church, as recorded in Scripture, alongside our present modes of church.

Ezra did that at the water gate. Jesus did it in his hometown synagogue in Luke 4. In exilic conditions, the Word gathers a people. This is Israel in Diaspora: the people listen, aligning themselves to the word, singing the Songs of Zion, naming the name, telling the story, and thus survive as God's people.

> By the rivers of Babylon—
>> there we sat down and there
>>> we wept
>> when we remembered Zion. . . .
>
> For there our captors
>> asked us for songs,
> and our tormentors asked for mirth, saying,
>> "Sing us one of the songs of Zion!"
>
> How could we sing the LORD's song
>> in a foreign land?
> If I forget you, O Jerusalem,
>> let my right hand wither! (Psalm 137:1, 3-5)

I believe that exile is not too strong a term with which to characterize the current social location of the North American church. Stanley Hauerwas and I suggested this in our *Resident Aliens: Life in the Christian Colony,* where we said that to the church has been given the task of being "an alternative *polis,* a countercultural social structure called the church . . . , something that the world is not and can never be."[6] Most of Israel's Scripture was written by a community either in exile or coming out of exile, Scripture like that found in Nehemiah. Only exilic literature could adequately express the pain and the loss felt by disestablished, relinquished Israel in the catastrophe of exile. Yet some of Israel's most assertive, visionary, hopeful, pushy poetry and prose was also written in exile, testimony to Israel's great faith in the reign of a resourceful God who is determined to have a people. To understand how a defeated, displaced people could still express evangelical chutzpah in the face of Babylonian imperialism, one would have to know a God who tends toward the oppressed. Think of all of our biblical interpretation and study as our attempt to "sing the Lord's song in a strange land."

When John the Baptizer was challenged by authorities, John told them that God is able to raise up a people out of the stones in the Jordan if need be, if God's chosen ones will not listen, will not repent and return. God is determined to have a family. God's way of making a people is through the Word, through preaching like that of John, through promises (Luke 3:1-21). It's Genesis 1 all over again.

The church is gathered by the Word. In just a few centuries, the church defeated Rome on the basis of nothing more than this rather disordered collection of writings called Scripture. By Water and the Word, God constitutes a family, the church. And pastors have the function of helping the church in exile read, reflect, and embody the Word of God. Our God is loquacious, creating the world with nothing more than words. Every time God's word is uttered, new worlds come into being that would be otherwise unavailable without the gift of the Word.

> By faith we understand that the world was created by the word of God, so that what is seen was made out of things which do not appear. (Hebrews 11:3 RSV)

The Authority of the Word

When a sermon is preached, it is based on an external authorization. The integrity of the preacher, the preacher's rhetorical gifts, and the setting of the sermon in the liturgy may all be possible sources of homiletical authority. Yet none of these sources of authority is as significant as Scripture. Christian preaching has always been biblical preaching. Our earliest sermons in Acts and bits of sermons in Paul's letters all show that gospel speakers do not begin in the present, in the speaker's experience, or in an astute assessment of the current situation. They begin with the Bible, with citation of and remembrance of Scripture. Jesus spoke of that wise scribe who brings forth from the treasure of the tradition that which is old and that which is new (Matthew 13:52). That's what biblical preachers do.

Although individual preachers may have various theologies of scriptural inspiration depending upon their church tradition, their own dealings with Scripture, and their biases, all preachers generally begin with the assumption that the Bible is a gift of God that uniquely illuminates human life in the present and that uniquely, indispensably speaks the promises of God and the truth that is God in Jesus Christ. Therefore it is a homiletical truism that the first step in preparing a Christian sermon is encounter with a biblical text.

In our encounters with the biblical text, we preachers are in conversation with an honored senior colleague whose testimony is more trustworthy than our own. As we have said, Scripture itself is homiletical in intent. Therefore a preacher will tend to feel a kinship with someone like Mark, marveling at Mark's range of metaphor and style, the sly way in which Mark arranges his material and the surprising twists and turns of his rhetoric. We preachers will therefore see things in Scripture that more prosaic readers of the text—such as professors of religion in college religion departments—tend to miss.

The preacher will approach Scripture with the presupposition that a given text wants to be not just the Word of God in the abstract, a written word lying dead on a page, but the Word of God now, in today's congregation. The preacher is not approaching the ancient biblical text as if the preacher were analyzing Homer in order to do a report on the *Iliad*, desperately hoping to make this ancient writing relevant to a contemporary audience. The preacher goes to the text with the assumption that here is a primary locus for the work of the Holy Spirit and that here the living, resurrected Christ intends to be with his people, here, now. Scripture is God in action, not just then but also now.

We enter into this strange new world of the Bible with eagerness, with respect, as we might wade into a swirling, fast-moving, unfathomably deep river, a river that we want to experience and enjoy rather than simply dam up, control, and channel. We realize that we are entering a difficult and demanding world, not because the Bible is ancient and Jewish but because it is a world that is based upon convictions and assumptions (i.e., Jesus Christ is Lord) quite different from our own.

In beginning a sermon on Genesis, Origen, that third-century homiletical genius who helped Christianity conquer a pagan world, compares the interpreter of Scripture to a sailor in a small boat who is borne onto a great sea by the winds of the Holy Spirit. He admits that the preaching of Scripture such as Genesis can be tough sailing. And yet,

> The further we progress in reading, the greater grows the accumulation of mysteries for us. And just as if someone should embark on the sea borne by a small boat, as long as he is near the land he has little fear. But when he has advanced little by little into the deep and has begun either to be lifted on high by the swelling waves or brought down to the depths by the same gaping waves, then truly great fear and terror permeate his mind because he has entrusted a small craft to such immense waves. So we also seem to have suffered, who small in merits and slight in ability, dare to enter so vast a sea of mysteries. But if by your prayers the Lord should see fit to give us a favorable breeze of his Holy Spirit we shall enter the port of salvation with a favorable passage of the word.[7]

Perhaps this is why we speak of a "passage" of Scripture, because so many times for us a text has been a vessel that has carried us from one place to another, a door that opened to us, leading us into a new existence.

The New Testament speaks of "preaching" with a variety of words—the act of proclamation (*keryssein*), the announcement of good news (*euangelizesthai*), conversing (*homilien*), witnessing (*martyrein*), teaching (*didaskein*), prophesying (*propheteuein*), and exhorting (*parakalein*). All have their roots in the peculiar speech of the synagogue, in the confrontation that occurred there between God's people and God's word (Acts 13:16-41). Whereas classical rhetoric fashioned public speeches in conformity to the rhetoric of the empire, Christian speaking arose out of the peculiar and manifold intentions of the biblical text. Whereas classical rhetoricians such as Aristotle spent much of their energies concerned with the limitations and desires of the listeners, urging speakers to take care to tailor their speeches to the disposition of their listeners, Christian speaking is first concerned with the disposition of the biblical text and its power, through the Holy Spirit, to evoke the hearers it deserves before it troubles itself about the desires and deficiencies of those who hear or refuse to hear. The biblical preacher proclaims as the text proclaims, confident that the text is still quite capable of evoking a good hearing, despite the limits of either the preacher or the listeners. The Christian preacher is so much more interested in the nature of the God who is to be brought to speech rather than the nature of the listeners who are to hear the speech or in the limits or attributes of the speaker who must give the speech. Or as Acts sometimes says it, the Word of God is so lively, interesting, and explosive that, even through our pitiful efforts, by the grace of God, "The word of the Lord grew mightily and prevailed" (Acts 19:20). "The word of God continued to spread; the number of the disciples increased greatly. . . ." (Acts 6:7).

A sermon begins in encounter with the biblical text. As preachers, we do not rummage about in other texts until we have done business with this privileged text, until we have prayerfully, playfully, obediently attempted to listen to the text. This interpretive work is done on behalf of the congregation. The preacher is the one who is ordained by the church to engage in listening to the text in behalf of the church, listening to the church so that the preacher might listen with them to the text. Preachers are sometimes characterized as great talkers. But if we are effective and faithful, we are actually great listeners. Bonhoeffer speaks of listening as a holy act:

> Christians, especially ministers, so often think that they must always contribute something when they are in the company of others, that this is one service that we have to render. They forget that listening can be a greater service than speaking.

Many people are looking for an ear that will listen. They do not find it among Christians, because these Christians are talking when they should be listening. But the one who can no longer listen to his brother or sister will soon no longer be listening to God either. . . . This is the beginning of death of the spiritual life, and in the end there is nothing left but spiritual chatter and clerical condescension arrayed in pious words.[8]

Think of all of our skills of biblical interpretation as skills in service of faithful listening to the text, as practices of prayer. It is enough for other Christians to encounter the Bible in order that they grow in their personal relationship with Christ. The pastor bears the burden of listening on behalf of the whole church.

In our encounters with Scripture in preparation for preaching, we do not come to the Scripture with the assumption that we stand in a privileged, enlightened, modern world and therefore ask questions of an archaic, naive, primitive world of the Bible. It is better to think of the Bible questioning us rather than our questioning the Bible. "Lord, you have searched me and known me," says the psalmist. We must read the Bible in such a way that the Bible is allowed to read us, to interpret our world in the light of the reign of God in Jesus Christ. "Adam, where are you?" the Lord asked our first ancestor in the Garden of Eden. So our primary questions may not be, "Is this biblical material relevant to me?" but rather, "How can we better align our lives to the demands of Scripture?" Not, "Does this passage address my needs as a twenty-first-century person who uses a fax machine?" but rather, "How does this passage rearrange and judge our notions of our needs?" The burden of Scripture is also a blessing that relieves us of the pointless burdens that this society places upon our backs.

Sermons are our homiletical attempt to get the sermon off the printed page and into an oral form. Some preachers are prejudiced against concerning themselves greatly with matters of style and delivery. Their theology of preaching tells them that the truth of God is self-evident, needing no fancy frills or rhetorical presentation. This attitude overlooks the considerable range and skill of biblical communicators who, in the Scriptures, utilize remarkable literary creativity and diversity in their presentation of God. In preaching, style is substance, the way the truth is presented is part of the truth. Just as we cannot boil a parable of Jesus down to one abstract idea without losing much of the force of the parable, so we cannot simply list a series of good ideas and have proclamation of the gospel. Sometimes preachers spend so much energy in their biblical exegesis and initial study and preparation of what they are going to say in a sermon that they have no time or energy left for struggling with *how* they are to say a sermon. In most studies of lay reaction to preaching, issues of style and delivery are foremost in the listeners' minds, perhaps because our listeners instinctively know that style and delivery are integrally related to biblical substance and content. When they say after a sermon, "That was a good enough talk, but it just wasn't a sermon," what they usually mean is they have been subjected to an artless, cold presentation rather than an announcement of good news. The preacher stands up to speak as the herald who bears news that stays news because it is the good news that is essential for our salvation.

The preacher will find it helpful to assume that, in interpreting Scripture, these writings have an exclusively theological purpose. The biblical preacher's great hermeneutical principle is this: Scripture always and everywhere tends to speak primarily about God and then only secondarily or derivatively about us. The Bible is about more significant tasks than providing us with principles for daily life, rules for happier homes, meaning for our vacuous lives. The Bible speaks always and everywhere about God.

Scripture is God's true story. It not only tells the truth about God but also renders the true God truly with us. The God thereby rendered is not the product of fertile ancient imaginations, not a projection of the highest and best aspirations of human spiritual striving, not some mythic figuration of the human psyche. This God is the stranger who comes to us and speaks to us Luther's "external word." If not, then we would have had absolutely no means of knowing this God. The primary agent of Scripture is God; the author of Scripture is God; the concern of Scripture is God. This suggests that our toughest challenge in reading the Bible today is not that it is ancient and written in foreign tongues but rather that we live in a narcissistic, self-obsessed culture that has a myriad of ways of deluding us into thinking that we can be gods unto ourselves. It will be a reach for us to get out of ourselves and get interested in something other than ourselves. In such a cultural setting, the biblical preacher's highest task will be to get us to look at God rather than ourselves.

To be sure, in speaking about God, Scripture often has important implications for us. But those implications tend to be secondary and derivative of the main task of attempting to reveal God. Too much contemporary preaching appears to have forsaken this theological purpose for biblical interpretation in favor of essentially anthropological concerns. These sermons usually begin with the preacher's amateurish assessment of the contemporary human condition—we are depressed, or we are searching for meaning in life, or we are frightened about the future—then the preacher rummages about in the Bible and finds there some principle or insight that can be applied to the contemporary human condition, usually something that the congregation is to think or do in order to set themselves right.

This essentially anthropological, Pelegian, human-centered use of the Bible in sermons is unfortunate for a number of reasons. For one thing, we do not know what the "human condition" really is apart from a prior encounter with Jesus Christ. He defines our present situation, rather than our present situation defining him. Too often preaching becomes locked in a problem-solution format. The preacher presents some problem, some aspect of contemporary life that is, in the preacher's assessment, problematic. Then some insight from Scripture, the Christian tradition, church law, or commonsense wisdom is presented as the solution to this problem. In this sort of preaching, the Bible becomes a helpful resource, among others, for helping us with our problems. We and what we think are our problems become the purpose of preaching.

Among the theological problems with this approach to preaching is that the Bible does not simply want to speak to our world; the Bible wants to rock, transform, dismantle and recreate our world. The Bible tells us that we and our brilliant insights and earnest efforts are not the solution to our problems. The Bible does not simply want to help us better adjust to present circumstances, as the world defines our circumstances. The Bible wants to redeem us, save us, rescue and liberate us for life in a new world, a world that we would not have known about had not that new world been announced through preaching.

Preachers of the problem-solution ilk are often frustrated by the Bible's apparent lack of interest in so many of our pressing contemporary problems. They feel forced either to abandon Scripture as a source for their preaching or to twist and contort the biblical text to make it speak to our prior assessment of our contemporary context. I have thus heard sermons on "Better Family Life" based upon the parable of the prodigal son, a sermon on "Keeping Money in Its Place" based upon Jesus' call of the rich young man, or a sermon on economic justice based on Jesus' parable of the laborers in the vineyard. It is absurd trivialization of the gospel to think that Jesus told the parable of the prodigal son in order to foster happier families. Again, Scripture always and everywhere tends to speak first about God. So an appropriate hermeneutical question in encountering a biblical text is, "What does this text say about God?" or more actively, "How would God have me to change in order to make this text believable?"

Scripture has some peculiar notions of what our most pressing human problems are. For instance, amazingly little is said in Scripture about human sexuality. Jesus and his disciples present next to nothing said about their sexual interests, inclinations, or orientations. The conventional response to this curiosity is that Scripture was produced by naive, limited, first-century Jews who did not know that sexuality is the most interesting aspect of a human being—which is what we, in our advanced state of human development, now know.

Perhaps Scripture shows little interest in our sexual dilemmas, not because it is primitive and limited in its view of a human being but rather because it is working with a very different view of a human being, a view in which our sexuality is not the supreme defining characteristic of our humanity. Perhaps we, in our present notions of what is important and unimportant, are primitive and limited, not Scripture.

Scripture thinks that our greatest need is to be with the God who, in Jesus Christ, has shown such remarkable determination to be with us. A vision of God, rather than helpful hints for everyday living, is what Scripture seeks.

Speaking Like the Bible

Pastors, in our sermon preparation (is there any time in a pastor's day when the pastor is not, in a sense, preparing a sermon?), cultivate the virtues of humble, prayerful, obedient listening to Scripture. We discipline ourselves not to take a superior attitude toward the text. We nurture, in the words of Walter Brueggemann, an "obedient playfulness"[9] with the text, submitting to Scripture, willing to be judged and changed by the text, at the same time playfully delighting in the wonder, the weirdness, the sheer otherness of the text.

The pastor's interpretive duty can be a resource for pastoral audacity. To be forced through our daily reading and interpretation of Scripture to see ourselves not primarily as servants of the whims of the congregation but rather as servants of the demanding Word can be true pastoral freedom. We testify to what we have heard in Scripture. We speak, not out of our personal preferences or on the basis of our existential concern, but on the basis of what we have received in our pastoral encounter with Scripture. A congregation is more likely to hear our sermon on some controversial, difficult issue if it is clear that our sermon is based upon Scripture. We preach what we have been told to preach. We really believe that when we are encountered by Scripture, we are not simply encountering a set of interesting ideas about God, we are encountering the Risen Christ. We take such care with Scripture in our efforts to obey the voice at the

Transfiguration, "'This is my Son, the Beloved; with him I am well pleased; listen to him!'" (Matthew 17:5). Our scriptural interpretation is thus a form of prayer.

John Calvin called Scripture the "lens" through which Christians look at the world, the set of eyeglasses that brings things into focus. The biblical preacher attempts to talk like the Bible in order that the congregation might inculcate a scriptural way of construing the world. These ancient texts that comprise Scripture have a privileged place in our communication. Among the practical implications of these theological assertions are these:

1. Biblical preaching tends to be narrative rather than abstract, propositional, or theoretical because narrative is the typical biblical way of dealing with the truth of a trinitarian, incarnate God. There is something about story that is peculiarly suitable for the Bible's way with truth.

2. Biblical preaching often impresses the contemporary hearer as being strange, complex, and hard to understand. Few texts of Scripture have a single meaning limited to the intent of the original author. Scripture has multiple complex senses given by God, the author of the whole drama of salvation that we call "Scripture." Scripture tends to be "thick," multilayered, multivalent, and complex rather than univocal, monological, and "thin." Contemporary readers and listeners who have been formed by linear, reduced, more prosaic modes of communication (*USA Today*, government press releases, political sound bites, and even our very best sermons) can expect difficulty with the Bible's way of talking. They will need to pray for patience in their attempts to understand Scripture.

3. Because the Bible is so rich and diverse in its use of literary forms, biblical preaching will be similarly rich and diverse in its use of form. There is no "one size fits all" when it comes to biblical preaching forms. Few of

us preachers are as resourceful, imaginative, and risky as Scripture in its bold use of a wide array of literary devices in order to speak of Jesus Christ. So-called topical preaching, in which the preacher selects some topic for a sermon—a contemporary problem, some aspect of the human dilemma, a controversial ethical issue—is rarely biblical because topical preaching allows the world to set the boundaries and the goals of the conversation. Even so-called expository preaching —in which some biblical text is examined and then an idea is extracted from the text—is not truly biblical when the extracted idea is expounded and applied, turning biblical narrative into abstract, general concepts and principles.

4. The Bible's peculiar speech is not easily translated into terms that are readily available to the average contemporary audience. Favorite biblical words like *kingdom of God* or *salvation* have no readily available substitutes in the world's words. Therefore one of the tasks of preaching is the teaching of a new vocabulary and a new grammar whereby Christians are enabled truthfully to describe themselves and the world. Understanding of a sermon therefore requires conversion, formation, and indoctrination.

5. The world that the Bible renders through its stories, sagas, poetry, and hymns is more real than what passes for the "real world" among most of us. The preacher is to point to, submit to, and honor that world, obediently to serve the scriptural construal of reality before other imperial, conventional, or more socially acceptable definitions of reality. Part of the joy of being a biblical preacher is that we get a front-row seat at the spectacle of the creation of a new world. The Bible wants to give us new experiences, to create a new reality that would have been unavailable to us without the Bible. The Bible does not simply want to speak to the modern world. The Bible wants to change the

world, to create for us a world, through words, that would have been inaccessible to us without our submission to the text called Scripture.

To be a biblical preacher is to relish the delight of working with so thick, demanding, and resourceful a medium as Holy Scripture. It is to honor the Bible that we give it a privileged place in our communication. As a preacher, I am not free to rummage about in other sources, texts, or authorities before I have first done business with Scripture. I am to presume, in my sermon preparation, that these ancient Jews know more about God than I, that the world described by them in Scripture is more real, more relevant than any description of the world that I can come up with on my own or even with the help of *The New York Times*.

Which is to say that biblical preaching is part of the church's tough theological task of taking the Bible as God's word more seriously and ourselves a little less so.

CHAPTER FOUR

THE INCARNATE WORD

In the beginning was the Word, and the Word was with God, and the Word was God. He was in the beginning with God. All things came into being through him, and without him not one thing came into being. What has come into being in him was life, and the life was the light of all people. The light shines in the darkness, and the darkness did not overcome it. (John 1:1-5)

John's Gospel shuttles, almost immediately, from high-flown talk of "the Word" toward "a man sent from God, whose name was John" (1:6). So quickly we move from God to humanity, so swiftly the Word, the eternally begotten Word, becomes flesh, our flesh, as we are made to look at "a man sent from God, whose name was John." We are told little about this man whose name was John—nothing of his parentage or his hometown—only that he was "sent from God." In a way, that man is a parable for any preacher who has ever lived. The Fourth Gospel does not call him John the Baptist. It just calls him John.

John's main activity is preaching, and the location for his preaching is "the wilderness" (1:23), so the parable extends itself. This wild man addresses those who are in a wild, trackless, threatening waste of the wilderness. John was a forerunner of those who, like John Wesley, stood out on street corners or in open fields to preach. The Word goes out to those who need it most, out to the wilderness. John's location, his pulpit in the wilderness, reminds us that there are some words that are too true, too lively, to be fully contained in a temple, synagogue, or church. The Word of God is to be heard at these confined, established, sacred sites, to be sure. But the Word, the living Incarnate Word, cannot be contained. It reaches out, pushes out, even into the wilderness. The Word is greater even than the beautiful religious platforms that are built to present it.

The one sent from God has only one function: to "witness." A witness is someone who testifies, who simply tells what he or she has seen and heard. The witness is not to embellish or exaggerate. The witness has little significance in and of himself. His significance is in what the witness has to say about what the witness has seen and heard. We want an honest account of what the witness knows to be true. Except for two brief references to this "witness" (John 5:33-36; 10:40-42), these few verses are all that we hear of John. He speaks and then he disappears. When asked, "Who are you?" John replies that he is a "voice." He has no body, no substance or enduring significance other than the sound of a voice, a voice crying in the wilderness "that all might believe" (1:7).

The theologian Karl Barth says that John is the model for every preacher of every age. John is only interesting as a voice, a witness, someone who points toward the coming Christ. He is transparent, like a pane of glass, to the One who comes after him who is greater than he. As a witness, John is simply to testify to what he has seen and heard, no more. He must decrease as the One toward whom he points increases. His significance is not in himself but rather in the truth that he tells to those in the wilderness.

The Fourth Gospel says that Jesus is the Word (in the Greek, *logos*) who came down from heaven and dwelt among us. Although this is the only place in John's gospel where Jesus is called the Word, it is a powerful image of the Christ, a wonderful introduction to the significance of the Christ. As the Word, the Christ is God's self-communication, the major means of the establishment of divine-human communion. John says that the Eternal Word came to tent among us (that's what the verb "dwelt" literally means in the Greek, "pitched his tent among us") and his primary way of dwelling among us is as the Word (1:14). He was more than words can say, but never less than words. In Jesus, the words about God became God-in-the-flesh and dwelt among us as the Word. Jesus is God's Word to the world, God's sermon to us, God's Word to which all our words in all our sermons point. As Paul put it, "For what we preach is not ourselves, but Jesus Christ as Lord" (2 Corinthians 4:5 RSV). John's gospel employs a host of metaphors for Jesus—he is the door, the good shepherd, the vine, bread, water, life. But this great, vividly metaphoric Gospel begins with Jesus as the Word.

Something went wrong. The Word was uttered once again over the wasteland, over the dark chaos, the wilderness, and some heard and some did not. He came that they might receive him, believe in him, and thereby be empowered "to become children of God" (John 1:12 RSV), but it did not work out that way.

"His own . . . received him not" (John 1:11 RSV). This move from the Word, the eternal Word, coming down and dwelling among us to the subsequent rejection of the Word is a move that we shall see recapitulated a million times over in the preaching of the Word by a million voices in the wilderness. Generations of preachers will point, sometimes well, sometimes poorly, toward the One who is the Message that is mightier than his messengers, and those in the wilderness will shrug their shoulders or scratch their heads in mocking incomprehension and walk away. The story that John has to tell in the Fourth Gospel eventually leads to a cross.

The Word, by its very nature not self-evident, is prone to incomprehension and misunderstanding. Failure is everywhere for the Word. Throughout John's gospel, almost no one who is confronted by the Christ, the Word Made Flesh, understands anything he is talking about. He speaks to Nicodemus of being born of the water and Spirit, and the supposedly wise teacher thinks "birth." He speaks to the woman at the well of "living water come down from heaven," and she thinks water drawn up by a bucket. The Word is veiled, not easily accessible, hidden, arcane, and bewildering even as it is light, revelation, and present among us. Any preaching that is not at some moment also inaccessible, mysterious, and unfathomable is not a message about the Word Made Flesh. Any preacher who does not fail, and fail dramatically and often, to communicate the good news is not communicating the good news that is Jesus Christ. The preaching career of Jesus ended in failure on a cross.

Yet that end is not the end of the story (read John 20 and 21). John 1 is a reiteration of Genesis 1. The purposes of God for the Word are not forever stumped. The light shines in the darkness, and nothing that we have ever done, even the worst of it, has been able to overcome the light. To those who receive the Word has been given the gift to "become children of God" (1:12). "Blessed are those who have not seen yet believe," says the Risen Christ toward the end of John's gospel. Johannine irony is at work here all the way to the end: We have not seen Christ as his first followers saw him, and yet here we are, believing on the basis of nothing more than John's words about the Word. "These are written," says the Fourth Gospel, "that you may believe" (John 20:31 RSV). And despite all the setbacks and perfectly good reasons for not believing the testimony of a wild man with a voice like John's, we do.

Lecturing on preaching, in the little renegade seminary of the Confessing Church in Finkenwalde, Dietrich Bonhoeffer said, "For the sake of the proclaimed word the world exists with all of its words." In other words, God has given us Creation, not merely as the result of the creative Word but rather as that sphere that has been created to hear the Word, to be evoked continually by the Word. The purpose of the world and all its rich array of creatures, including us, is so that the Word might have an appropriate, grateful audience. "In the sermon the foundation for a new world is laid," says Bonhoeffer.[1] So every time a sermon is preached and heard, it's Genesis 1 and John 1 all over again. Light comes into the darkness, and the darkness never completely overcomes the light.

Incarnational Preaching

Bonhoeffer boldly linked preaching with the Word in the Flesh:

> The proclaimed word has its origin in the incarnation of Jesus Christ. It neither originates from a truth once perceived nor from personal experience. It is not a reproduction of a specific set of feelings. Nor is the word of the sermon the outward form of the substance which lies behind it. The proclaimed word is the incarnate Christ himself . . . the thing itself. The preached Christ is both this Historical One and the Present One. . . . He is the access to the historical Jesus. Therefore the proclaimed word is not a medium of expression for something else, something which lies behind it, but rather it is Christ himself walking through his congregation as the word.[2]

When Jesus walks through his congregation in the words of the sermon as the Word, the congregation experiences Jesus as God in the Flesh. Jesus Christ is the self-attestation, the self-proclamation, the self-revelation of God. Christians are those who claim that, when we hear of the life, death, and teaching of this Jew from Nazareth who lived briefly, died violently, and rose unexpectedly, we have heard as much of God as we ever hope to hear. God was so fully present in Jesus the Christ, in the flesh, incarnate, reconciling the world to himself, that early Christian writings like John's gospel just quite naturally called him, "The Word."

> In many and various ways God spoke of old to our fathers by the prophets; but in these last days he has spoken to us by a Son. (Hebrews 1:1-2 RSV)

The Incarnation, the Word Made Flesh, is the supreme example of God's determination, from the beginning of the world, to be with us no matter what it takes. Jesus the Christ is fully human and fully divine, without any subordination or mixing of either the human or the divine. Jesus was not "the greatest person who ever lived," not "a great moral example," not a wonderfully insightful peripatetic wisdom teacher. He was God in the flesh. It was not that the disciples encountered Jesus as a wonderful person then, after his death, got all worked up in their grief and began thinking, "He is almost like a God." It was rather that, when they encountered Jesus, particularly as they encountered him after his resurrection, everything fell into place, their eyes were opened, and they were able to say with one voice, "You are the Messiah, the Son of God!"

At the same time, he was not some divine automaton, dropping down out of heaven, moving like a hard-wired robot to his predetermined death, an angelic being for whom his human form was only apparent. He was the enfleshment of God. His human life was not some fleshly husk that he could discard once his divinity took over his humanity. He never got over being fully human while he was fully divine. The Incarnation is the great mystery of God being veiled and unveiled, near yet distant, human yet divine, understandable yet mysterious, divine yet human, God Almighty tenting among us as the Word. Sometimes we had difficulty hearing him because of his humanity—God so near to us, as a Suffering Servant, that it was hard to imagine. Sometimes we had difficulty hearing him because of his divinity—God whose ways and thoughts were more strange and distant from us than we had imagined. Sometimes we heard him precisely because of his humanity—God so near as to be unavoidable. And sometimes we heard him precisely because of his divinity—God revealing to us that which we could not hear except as a gift of God. Everyone who speaks of this Incarnate One will find that his or her speaking participates in this same veiling and unveiling that characterized the Word Made Flesh.

The Incarnation is the great mystery that makes preaching possible. As we have stressed earlier, preaching is a divinely wrought, miraculous act. Preaching is God's speech. Preaching is God's chosen means of self-revelation. If a sermon "works," it does so as a gracious gift of God, a miracle no less than the virginal conception of Jesus by the Holy Spirit. One reason why Christians tend to believe in the likelihood of miracles like the virgin birth of Jesus or the resurrection of Christ is that we have experienced miracles of a similar order, if not similar magnitude, in our own lives as we have listened to a sermon. Something has come to us from afar; something has been born in us that we ourselves did not conceive. A word has been heard that is not self-derived. It's a mysterious, undeserved gift. It's a miracle. Thus preaching is theological not only in its substance but also in its means. Preaching is not only talk about God but miraculous talk by God.

At the same time preaching is an utterly human, mundane, carnal, and fleshly thing. Bonhoeffer says, "The proclaimed word is the Christ bearing human nature. This word is . . . the Incarnate One who bears the sins of the world. . . . The word of the sermon intends to accept mankind, nothing else. It wants to bear the whole human nature."[3] Even for Almighty God to speak to us, and to speak in ways that we comprehend, is an incarnational exercise. Aristotle defined a human being as a "word using animal." For God to speak words to us animals, to become embodied in the words of Scripture or a sermon or the words of the Risen Christ, is for God to condescend to us, to stoop, to take up our nature, to risk enfleshment. A less secure, less sovereign and free godlet might have kept silent rather than risk intercourse with us on our level. To talk with us is to take up the sins of the world, to risk entanglement in our sinful evasion of the truth. If Christ has not preached to us, presumably we would have little reason to crucify him. His sermons, in a sense, brought out the worst in us. He told us the truth about God, and we hated him for it.

Conversation is always a risk that too much might be given away in the course of an attempt to be understood by the other, power might be given over to the other, too much might be revealed in the course of the conversation. This God talks to us and dares to give us God's name so that we, even in our humanity, might call upon God, might invoke the name that is above all other names (Philippians 2). It is the supreme testimony to the true greatness of this God that, in the Incarnation, this God stoops. God makes room among us as the Word.

Thou dost beset me behind and before, and layest thy hand upon me. Such knowledge is too wonderful for me; it is high, I cannot attain it. Whither shall I go from thy Spirit? Or whither shall I flee from thy presence? (Psalm 139:5-7 RSV)

A sermon is a divine act. It is an aspect of the true greatness of our God that our God stoops to us in the preached word. John Chrysostom (c. 347–407), called by his hearers "The Golden Tongued," speaks eloquently and frequently of the Incarnation as God's glorious "condescension" that makes possible our deification. God loves us so much, said Chrysostom, that God came down among us and talked our talk, walked our walk, so that we, even in our limited understanding, might know God. God spoke to us in a manner that fit our limitations. Revelation is linked to graciousness. We know about God, we hear God's Word only as a gift of a gracious God. In a wonderful sermon on Genesis 3:8, Chrysostom speaks of the gracious way in which "they heard the sound of the LORD God walking in the garden." Chrysostom notes that it is a wonderful God who risks all and dares to stroll beside us in the garden, uttering things to us that we can understand, getting down on our level.

The Incarnation stresses that a sermon is a human activity. It can be, by God's grace, God's Word; but it is not God's Word pristinely handed over to us for our control and usage. The preacher is the one who bears, in the words of Paul, "treasure in an earthen vessel" (from 2 Corinthians 4:7). The gospel is the treasure that is born in sometimes broken, weak, cracked, and limited human vessels that are unworthy of such content. Thus, in preaching, the Word of God is both revealed and arcane, unveiled and veiled. Hearing is never self-evident, rarely obvious or direct, but mediated, tainted, and constrained by the human limits of both the preacher and the congregation.

We preachers must therefore pray that God will give us as great a gift of critical self-knowledge as possible. It is demanded of all of us preachers that we be willing to engage in a lifetime of self-reflection, self-criticism, and self-discovery so that we might better know all the ways that we adulterate the Word of God in our words. Every word I preach is not God's word; sometimes I speak out of my own human striving, self-pity, self-justification, and defensiveness. I need to learn as much as I can about my mixed motives for preaching what I preach. I must carefully note all those biblical texts that bring out the worst in me and those congregational situations in which I am not to be fully trusted as a servant of the Word. I must confess all the ways in which I get in the way of God's word in a sermon and fail to be, like John the Baptist, the one who points to the Christ rather than a substitute for Christ.

I once read through a folder of my first sermons that were preached during my first year as a pastor. The majority of these sermons in some way or another criticized the then current war in Vietnam, excoriating President Nixon for his leadership of the country even though Richard Nixon was never present to hear any of these sermons.

Reflection upon these sermons suggested to me that they were preached for motivations other than the edification, comfort, or correction of my congregation. Those sermons said much more about me and my needs, my continuing adolescent authority problems, my self-styled "prophetic preaching," than the demands of the gospel.

I once heard a preacher begin a sermon, with great drama and more than a trace of theatrics, saying, "It is very hard for me to say what I feel I must say to you today in my sermon."

One elderly woman in the pew in front of me leaned over and whispered just loud enough for all those seated around to hear, "I bet it's not that hard for him to say this."

When the gospel moves out beyond the boundaries between Jews and Gentiles, and Peter is driven toward the house of the Roman centurion, Cornelius, the pagan is surprised to see this leader of the church coming to his home. In great gratitude Cornelius falls to his feet and worships Peter. (These pagan, governmental, military sorts tend to worship just about anything if given half a chance to worship something.) Peter rebukes him saying, "Stand up; we are human beings like yourselves"

(Acts 10:26 author paraphrase). Time and again, preachers must remind themselves and our hearers that as we stand before our congregations and preach, we are human beings, too.

An incarnational faith implies that, as a human being who is sometimes given God's word to speak, I must honor the body that God has given me to use in this ministry. Preaching an incarnational faith means that preaching is a physical as well as a spiritual act. A preacher who stands up to preach on Sunday without adequate rest and preparation has not only committed a theological error but a moral lapse as well. Good preaching requires prayer, the inspiration of the Holy Spirit, intelligence, and charm; but it also requires hard work. I expect that many preachers fail at the task not because God is not graciously self-giving but rather because the preacher is undisciplined. Many sermons fail not because of some strictly theological infidelity on the part of the preacher but rather because of a failure of time and energy devoted to the task of constructing the sermon, which is, in light of the Incarnation, a theological failure.

My voice is my God-given instrument. I must practice good stewardship of that voice. I heard an old preacher tell how every Sunday morning he sat at a piano in the parsonage and sang the musical scale repeatedly in order to prepare his voice for the sermon. I once took pride that I was not the sort of preacher who needed to curtail Saturday evening socializing in order to preach well on a Sunday. Then I got older and had to honestly come to terms with my physical limits. As a result, I am home earlier on a Saturday evening. As preachers, we are not angels or disembodied spirits, but we are "human beings like yourselves." God has created no human being to be a limitless, eternally energetic, perpetually young being but rather to be a finite creature.

As noted earlier, Karl Barth said that the ideal sermon is to be like a polished pane of glass that we look through to God. But Barth's transparency metaphor for the sermon breaks down when viewed in the light of an incarnational faith. The Incarnation does not obliterate our humanity but rather uses it, fulfills it, commandeers it for divine purposes. Jesus did not just appear to suffer humanly and die on the cross (the Docetist heresy); he really suffered, bled, and died on the cross. One cannot separate the human form from the divine presence and end up with an incarnate God. Nor can one peel away the rhetorical form of the sermon from the divine intent of the sermon and still have the Word Made Flesh.

So the Incarnation implies that we preachers are not concerning ourselves with trivialities when we consider the design, form, arrangement, and structure of a sermon or when we agonize over issues of delivery and presentation of a sermon. A sermon is not a series of exalted, detached, spiritual ideas in disembodied form with the ideas being the only matters of substance in the sermon. The Word of God did not appear as a universal human being, anywhere and anytime. The Eternal Word was incarnate as a Jew from Nazareth. The form of his incarnation was not incidental to its meaning. We are not free, in an incarnational faith, to act as if the real significance of a sermon is in some inner, spiritual, ethereal idea that is contained in a disposable, expendable rhetorical husk. In a sermon, the Word takes flesh, our flesh, and is with us in a way that is a great credit to the determination of this God to be with us.

In our sermons, we preachers at times strain for connections, illustrations, stories, metaphors, and similes because of the Incarnation. In Jesus of Nazareth, we have experienced God among us in a way that is sacramental. Even as bread and wine become signs of God's self-giving, the Body and Blood of Christ as received in the congregation, so the sermon is a sort of sacrament of the Word. Here, standing before us in human form, living in a dusty place called Nazareth, is the great self-giving of God. We preachers long to connect the Word with the hearts and minds of our congregations because it is of the nature of this God to connect. Our pastoral care and pastoral visitation among our people is thus related to our preaching. The Christian faith is never some disembodied spiritual affair. The Word is meant to be heard, embodied, performed, and enfleshed. Bonhoeffer's most eloquent sermon was preached from the Nazi gallows.

Therefore we preachers, in our sermons, perform the word— seeking through our words, movements, gestures, and tone of voice to incarnate the biblical word—so that our congregations might embody the Word and the Word might dwell in them richly. That means that every sermon is meant to be a summons, a call, a vocation toward Incarnation. Some speaking, such as a lecture in a university classroom, is meant to be coolly considered, reflected upon, and thought through. The sermon is not of this genre. Through our illustrations, stories, references, and connections, we demonstrate that One who was fully God and fully human means fully to be with us as we are so that we might become as he is, so that the Word might be embodied even in us.

We preachers seek to perform the Word in our sermons so that the congregation might perform the Word in the world. As Paul told one of his troublesome congregations, "Now you are the body of Christ" (1 Corinthians 12:27). We preach in the awesome awareness that the church is, for better or worse, the physical form that the Risen Christ has chosen to take in the world. We preach to the Body so that it might be the Body of Christ.

A preacher is caught in that incarnational tension of having to speak a word for God but being utterly unable, by our humanity, to speak for God. The preacher must therefore stand up and proclaim in a resonant, strong voice, "Thus saith the Lord!" but at the same time confess with the young Isaiah, "Woe is me! I am a person of unclean lips and dwell among a people of unclean lips" (Isaiah 6:5 author paraphrase).

It is sad to hear a preacher who has sought prematurely to relax that incarnational tension by speaking as if, "these are just my ideas, my words, only my suggestions." False humility in preaching is a kind of veiled arrogance that proudly asserts its own vaunted humanity and refuses to bend one's life in service to the Word.

On the other hand, it is also sad to hear the preacher who speaks as if there is no tension, no human limitedness in preaching, the preacher who arrogantly acts as if God has given the Word in an unmediated, direct, spiritualized form that demands only assent from the congregation and needs no Resurrected Christ, no empowering Holy Spirit to make it work, no treasure for the earthen vessel to show that the glory belongs to God and not to us. We preachers are not free to speak without a note of tension in our voices—in polished and perfected oratory free of awkward gaps and pauses, dangling modifiers, and ragged conclusions—as if we have been given the last word on God, as if God has given over into our hands that sovereignty of revelation that only belongs to God. Like John the Baptist, we are only human beings sent from God to speak. Our voices fail, become overwhelmed, crack under the strain, and fade away; but the Word of the Lord endures forever. We can point to the Messiah, but we can in no way take the place of the Messiah as the substance or in the means of our preaching.

Trinitarian Preaching

It should not have been a surprise to us that Jesus as Emmanuel, God with us, was a preacher. It is of the nature of this God to be communicative, self-revealing, and epiphanic. Scripture is the long story of this God's attempt to be manifest to us. It is a story that begins with, "And God said . . ." and a relationship that begins with a question, "Adam, where are you?" It is a story that ends with the promise, "Behold, the dwelling place of God is with humanity. God will dwell with them and they shall be God's people" (Revelation 21:3 author paraphrase). The range and resourcefulness of this loquacious, determined-to-be-with-us God, as attested in Scripture, is rather amazing.

We refer to this God as Trinity—Father, Son, and Holy Spirit—which is not only a way of naming the complexity and richness of the One in whom we live, and move, and have our being (Acts 17) but also a way of pointing to God's very life as self-communication. The Gospels portray Jesus as the Son who is in constant communication with the Father, the Father as the One in constant interaction and revelation with the Son, and the Holy Spirit as incessantly empowering, thrusting, and moving in the lives of the Father and the Son as One. This divine inner self-communication of Father, Son, and Holy Spirit is so unremitting that we cannot speak of these three except as One.

The Fathers of the church, in pointing to the nature of the Trinity as active communication, spoke of the perichorietic nature of the Trinity (*perichoriesis*, literally, "to dance around"). Father, Son, and Holy Spirit never stop moving toward one another, moving around one another, in dynamic communion and interaction. It is not of the nature of this God to be silent, to be still, to refuse to communicate, to hold back and fail to give.

So when Paul says that "faith comes through hearing" he is testifying to what it is like to be in conversation with this steadfastly communicative God. It is of the nature of this God to communicate, first in the divine, inner, self-communication of the Trinity, then in the gracious overflowing of the constantly conversant Creator with all creatures. The Trinity, as speaking Creator, Redeemer, and Sustainer, is thus the means by which preaching occurs. We preachers cannot objectively describe and talk about this God because the Trinity is always self-revealing, speaking, and testifying to us through the Trinity's various modes of self-revelation.

One of the great challenges of the Trinitarian preacher is to do justice to the dynamic, perichoretic nature of the Trinity. We are not free to deal with "God" as a fixed concept, an eternal ideal, or a silent abstraction. God as Trinity is a constantly speaking subject, not a dead, static object. Oral communication, that is, preaching, is the basic nature of Christian communication because it is a uniquely suitable mode of discourse about a uniquely dynamic and communicative God. Scripture is a primary mode of Christian revelation, but even Scripture is secondary to preaching, which is more immediate, lively, and interactive than Scripture and more akin to Christ as the living, speaking subject rather than the dead, static object.

As we have noted, all Scripture was oral before it was written. The reception of the biblical word suffers today because it is nearly exclusively received as a written, printed word. As written, printed word, Scripture tends to look fixed on the page, obvious, immobile, and discernible. All we need to do is to focus upon the fixed, stationary word, analyze it, dissect it, parse it, and define it. The Christians produced by this limitation of revelation to the printed word tend, in my experience, to be static, frozen, and unimaginative because the only word they hear is that which is read. They would make better Muslims than Christians. Talking about a moving, dynamic, trinitarian God requires a supple, resourceful, well-modulated, and wide-ranging voice that is best reached in the spoken, rather than the written word.

This is one reason why the practice of providing Bibles in the pews of churches or asking individual Christians to bring their Bibles with them to church can be a limitation of Scripture. Christians are those who gather, with sisters and brothers in Christ, to hear God's word read, proclaimed, and enacted in community. Rather than following each word in their Bibles—heads down, eyes focused, imaginations limited—church people ought simply to be listening together to the power of the Word.

Another challenge of the Trinitarian, perichoretic preacher is to do justice to the complex, interactive, dynamic inner life of so interesting a God. A Trinitarian faith means that we are not free, as preachers, to focus exclusively upon the Father, extolling the virtues of a good, orderly, and beneficent Creator who has established a predictable and benign Creation; the Creation is also fallen and in need of redemption from its bondage to sin and death. We are not free to focus upon the Son to the exclusion of the Father, stressing only the atoning, redemptive, liberating work of the Savior; a good Creator has given us the good time and ordered place to live a daily life of praise and service in a world that is God's beloved Creation. Nor or we free to focus only upon the orderly, providential care of the Father and the redemptive, morally exemplary significance of the Son without also expecting the disrupting, prodding, renewing, and innovating work of the Holy Spirit. Still, we are not free to attempt to detach the Holy Spirit from the ethically demanding, life-in-this-world-now specific commands of the Son. The conventional three-point sermon, the sermon that explains, defines, and fixes is usually too tame and stable a medium for the dynamic, living Trinity. Most of us preachers require a three-year cycle of Scripture in the Common Lectionary combined with a minimum of fifty-two Sundays a year to do even proximate justice to so rich, multifaceted, and dynamic a God as the one named Trinity.

So the ultimate test of a sermon is not listener response, congregational reaction, or the preacher's own feelings about the sermon. The ultimate test is theological, specifically Trinitarian. Was this sermon about the God who meets us as Father, Son, and Holy Spirit?

John Wesley—when his lay preachers returned from their travels with tales of homiletical success, of hundreds converted, and of the formation of vibrant Christian enclaves in eighteenth-century England—usually found the opportunity to rise above a pragmatic and utilitarian assessment of preaching in order to ask of his preachers the theologically decisive, "But did you offer Christ?"

Preaching that aspires truthfully to speak of the Incarnate, Trinitarian God ought to desire no less than this.

CHAPTER FIVE

CROSS AND RESURRECTION IN PREACHING

I magine being asked to stand before a grand gathering of the good and the wise and being asked to make a speech about goodness, beauty, the meaning of life, the point of history, the nature of Almighty God, or some such high subject and having no material at your disposal but an account of a humiliating, bloody execution at a garbage dump outside a rebellious city in the Middle East. It is your task to argue that this story is the key to everything in life and to all that we know about God. This was precisely the position of Paul in Corinth. Before the populace of this cosmopolitan, sophisticated city of the empire, Paul had to proclaim that this whipped, bloody, scorned, and derided Jew from Nazareth was God With Us.

As Paul said, he had his work cut out for him because preaching about the cross "is folly to those who are perishing," foolishness and stupidity. A cross is no way for a messianic reign to end. Yet what else can this preacher say because, whether it makes sense to us or not, "it pleased God through the folly of what we preach to save those who believe" (1 Corinthians 1:18, 21 RSV).

Tailoring his manner of speech to his strange subject matter, Paul says that he chose a foolish sort of preaching that was congruent with his theological message:

When I came to you, brethren, I did not come proclaiming to you the testimony of God in lofty words or wisdom. For I decided to know nothing among you except Jesus Christ and him crucified. And I was with you in weakness and in much fear and trembling; and my speech and my message were not in plausible words of wisdom, but in demonstration of the Spirit and of power, that your faith might not rest in the wisdom of men but in the power of God. (1 Corinthians 2:1-5 RSV)

This is probably our earliest, most explicit statement on the peculiarity of Christian preaching and one of the few places in the New Testament where a preacher turns aside from the task of proclamation to discuss the nature of proclamation now that God has come as a crucified Messiah.

A crucified Messiah? It is an oxymoron, a violation of Israel's high expectations for a messianic liberator. In order to bring such a scandal to speech, Paul eschewed "lofty words or wisdom," the stock-in-trade of the classical orator. Rather than avoiding the scandal of the cross or attempting to sugarcoat its absurdity in order to make it more palatable, he limited his subject matter so that he knew, "nothing among you except Jesus Christ and him crucified." His manner of presentation, his delivery, was "weakness" and "fear and trembling," a rather peculiar demeanor for a public speaker. Why? So that nothing might move his hearers, nothing might convince them but "the power of God."

For God the Father to allow God the Son to be crucified, dead, and buried is for God to be pushed out beyond the limits of human expectation or human help. The cross is the ultimate dead end of any attempt at human self-fulfillment, human betterment, or progress. With Christ hanging from the cross, in humiliation and utter defeat, there is nothing to be done to vindicate the work of Jesus or to make the story come out right except "the power of God."

Paul says that he attempted to preach the gospel to the Corinthians in just that way. Rather than base his proclamation on human reason, common sense, or artful arguments, he spoke in halting, hesitant "fear and trembling" so that if they were to hear and to understand, to assent and to respond, it would have to be solely through "the power of God."

Paul says to the Corinthians that the cross is *moria,* moronic foolishness:

> For the message about the cross is foolishness to those who are perishing, but to us who are being saved it is the power of God. For it is written,
>
> "I will destroy the wisdom of the wise,
>   and the discernment of the discerning I will thwart."
>
> Where is the one who is wise? Where is the scribe? Where is the debater of this age? Has not God made foolish the wisdom of the world? For since, in the wisdom of God, the world did not know God through wisdom, God decided, through the foolishness of our proclamation, to save those who believe. For Jews demand signs and Greeks desire wisdom, but we proclaim Christ crucified, a stumbling block to Jews and foolishness to Gentiles, but to those who are the called, both Jews and Greeks, Christ the power of God and the wisdom of God. For God's foolishness is wiser than human wisdom, and God's weakness is stronger than human strength. (1 Corinthians 1:18-25)

Cruciform Preaching

A cruciform faith requires a peculiar way of preaching that is foolishness to the world. When the speaker points to Jesus hanging helplessly on the cross and says, "Jesus Christ is Lord!" the predictable audience reaction is, "Why? How?"

Then the speaker is tempted to offer assorted evidence for such a patently ridiculous claim: citations from religious authorities, illustrations from everyday life, personal experience, and connections with the presuppositions of the audience. Classical rhetoric said that there were three means of persuasion of an audience: reason, emotions, and the character of the speaker.

Note that Paul, in writing to the Corinthians about the folly of his preaching, rejects all of these classical means of persuasion, perhaps because there is no way for a speaker to get us from here to there, from our expectations for God to God on a cross, by conventional means of persuasion. When asked, "What is your evidence for your claim?" Paul simply responds, "the Cross." What else can he say? The cross so violates our frames of reference, our means of sorting out the claims of truth, that there is no way to get there except by "demonstration of the Spirit" and by "the power of God." The only way for preaching about the cross to "work" is as a miracle, a gift of God.

To underscore the miraculous quality of cruciform Christian proclamation, Paul said that he spoke "in weakness and in much fear and trembling"—hardly what we would expect from an adept speaker. Yet Paul says he preached thus to show that nothing—neither the eloquence of the speaker nor the reasoning powers of the hearers—could produce faith in a crucified savior except the "power of God."

Those who would preach the cross are forced to live with the homiletical implications of a crucified God:

1. Luther was fond of contrasting a "theology of glory," in which the cross was seen as avoidable, optional equipment for Christians, a mere ladder by which we climb up to God, with a "theology of the cross" that, according to Luther, calls things by their proper names and is unimpressed with most that impresses the world. A theology of glory preaches the cross as just another technique for getting what we want whereas a theology of the cross proclaims the cross as the supreme sign of how God gets what God wants. The cross is a statement that our salvation is in God's hands, not ours, that our relationship to God is based upon something that God suffers and does rather than

upon something that we do. To bear the cross of Christ is to bear its continual rebuke of the false gods to which we are tempted to give our lives. Auto-salvation is the lie beneath most theologies of glory. When self-salvation is preached, reducing the gospel to a means for saving ourselves—by our good works, or our good feelings, or our good thinking—then worldly wisdom and common sense are substituted for cruciform gospel foolishness and blasphemy is the result.

2. The cross is a reminder that there is no eloquent, rhetorically savvy way by which we can ascend to God. All of our attempts to climb up to God are our pitiful efforts at self-salvation. God descends to our level by climbing on a cross, opening up his arms, and dying for us, because of us, with us. Paul's thoughts on the foolishness of preaching that avoids "lofty words of wisdom" suggests that Christian rhetoric tends to be simple, restrained, and direct—much like the parables of Jesus. The Puritans developed what they called the "plain style" of preaching out of a conviction that Christian speech ought not to embellish, ought not to mislead hearers into thinking that there was some way for a sermon to work in the hearts and minds of the hearers apart from the gift of the Holy Spirit that makes sermons work.

3. Christian theology has always affirmed that the cross is not only a window through which we see the true nature of God as the embodiment of suffering love but also the truthful mirror in which we see ourselves. Cruciform preaching can't help speaking of our sin. Jesus was nailed to the wood on the basis of a whole host of otherwise noble human ideals and aspirations like law and order, biblical fidelity, and national security. Preaching offers the grace of God along with a good dose of honesty about the human condition, honesty that we would not have had without the

cross. After Calvary we could no longer argue that we are, down deep, basically good people who are making progress once we get ourselves organized and enlightened. The cross is also a reminder that Jesus' preaching was brutally rejected and if our preaching is about Jesus, then it will often be rejected as well. There is no way to talk about gospel foolishness without risking rejection. Preachers therefore ought to be more surprised when a congregation gratefully understands, receives, and inculcates our message rather than when it misunderstands, rejects, and ignores our message. "We are fools for the sake of Christ" (1 Corinthians 4:10).

4. Preaching Jesus can be a perilous vocation. One of the first great Christian sermons was by Stephen who, for his homiletical efforts, was stoned to death (Acts 7–8). Christian preachers not only talk like Jesus but sometimes suffer and die like Jesus. Jesus was upfront in saying that the cross is not optional equipment for discipleship: "If anyone wants to follow after me, let him deny himself and take up his cross and follow me. For whoever wants to save his life will lose it, and whoever loses his life for my sake and for the sake of the gospel will save it" (Mark 8:34-35 author paraphrase). When this episode is reported by Luke (9:18-26), Jesus goes on to relate cross-bearing to "me and . . . my words" (v. 26). Sometimes, the particular, peculiar cruciform burden that preachers must bear is the words of Jesus. The cross is not some chronic illness, not some annoying person. The cross is that which is laid upon us because we are following a crucified savior and, for us preachers, having to proclaim the words of this savior can be quite a burden. For Paul, the cross is not only something that God does to and for the world, unmasking the world's gods, exposing our sin, forgiving our sin through suffering love, but also the cross is the pattern for Christian life. He could say, "I

have been crucified with Christ; and it is no longer I who live, but it is Christ who lives in me. And the life I now live in the flesh I live by the faith of the Son of God, who loved me and gave himself for me" (Galatians 2:19-20, as translated in the NRSV footnote). And yet, the good news is that his yoke is easy and his burden is light, which is to say as burdensome and difficult as Jesus and his words can be, they are less burdensome and more fun than most of the other burdens the world tries to lay on our backs.

5. The cross is a story about the obedience of Christ, obedience even unto death. A faithful preacher's life will be characterized by obedience to the task of proclaiming a foolish (by the world's standards of wisdom) gospel. Preachers must discipline their lives so that there is no time in the pastoral week when a sermon is not in process, when the pastor is not wrestling with the biblical text and the demands of the congregational context. Preaching is hard work, requiring the cultivation of a host of skills that are difficult to develop. If we are called to preach (and who would take up this task without being called to do it?) then we must be obedient enough to the vocation to work at it. I believe the roots of clerical sloth are theological rather than primarily psychological. We become lazy and slovenly in our work because we have lost the theological rationale for the work.

6. Yet to take up the cross of Christ, to be willing to assume a yoke of obedience upon our shoulders, oblivious to the praise or blame of our congregations, is also the basis of what it means to have life and that abundantly, to live one's life in the light of true glory come down from heaven in the person of Jesus the Christ. As gospel preachers, preaching in the shadow of the cross, we get to talk about something and someone more important than ourselves. We get to proclaim Christ and him crucified, a rebuke to the world's

means of salvation, the great promise to a world dying for the truth. We get to expend our lives in work more significant than the lies by which most of the world lives. Working with a crucified God is a great adventure, a risky, perilous, wonderful undertaking and so much more interesting than mere servility to the wisdom of the world. Every time someone is confronted by the cross of Christ and hears, believes, responds; every time someone is liberated from enslavement to the world's false promises, then the preacher can take great satisfaction that the promises of God are indeed true, that God graciously continues, in us preachers and our sermons, to choose and to use "what is foolish [*moria*] in the world to confound the wise" (1 Corinthians 1:27 author translation).

Resurrection Preaching

Paul says that a Christian is someone who says that Jesus Christ was crucified and then raised from the dead (Romans 10:9). The cross did not erase the suffering of Jesus but rather completed it, became the means whereby God vindicated the crucified Jesus. Here is God's great vindication of Jesus, "The God of our fathers raised Jesus whom you killed by hanging him on a tree. God exalted him at his right hand as Leader and Savior, to give repentance to Israel and forgiveness of sins" (Acts 5:30-31 RSV). In the Resurrection, it was as if God said, "This is who I am. This is my way with the world—suffering, forgiving, triumphing love."

In a curious passage, Paul links the Resurrection with preaching and preaching with Resurrection:

Now I would remind you, brethren, in what terms I preached to you the gospel, which you received, in which you stand, by which you are saved. . . . For I delivered to you as of first importance what I also received, that

73

Christ died for our sins in accordance with the scriptures, that he was buried, that he was raised on the third day in accordance with the scriptures, and that he appeared. . . . . Now if Christ is preached as raised from the dead, how can some of you say that there is no resurrection of the dead? But if there is no resurrection of the dead, then Christ has not been raised; if Christ has not been raised, then our preaching is in vain and your faith is in vain. (1 Corinthians 15:1, 3-5, 12-14 RSV)

Some at Corinth are denying the Resurrection. What proof do they have that Jesus truly arose from the dead and appeared to his first followers? In response, Paul says that they know that Christ is raised because that's what Paul preached to them. Is that all? Listen to Paul's logic, "I have preached to you that Christ is raised from the dead. Now if I preached that, how can some of you say there is no resurrection of the dead?"

Paul goes on to say, in effect, "Now if there is no resurrection of the dead then Christ has not been raised and that would mean that, when I preached, I lied and that your faith is in vain. But I did tell the truth in my preaching, and just to prove it, I'm going to preach it to you again. 'Christ has been raised from the dead.'" There.

Tom Long asks, "What sort of circular, merry-go-round logic is this? We want proof of Easter and all Paul gives us is more preaching? 'I told you about the Resurrection. You don't believe in the Resurrection? Let me tell you about the Resurrection.'"[1] Logicians say this is an "if this-then this" sort of logic. If X is true, then Y must be true. Such arguments are dependent upon their ability to touch down somewhere in irrefutable human experience. The first proposition must be true. If not, the second proposition is false. If X is not irrefutably true, then there is no way that Y can be true. "If your roommate is now asleep in the dorm," then "she cannot be here in Chapel." For the logic to work, I need some proof backing the first proposition in the chain. "Ann, call 555-9192 and see if Sue Smith's roommate answers." That would provide irrefutable truth to the first claim.

"Yep, she's asleep in the dorm," therefore she is not here at the Chapel.

Our logic moves deductively beginning with what we know for sure (She is asleep in the dorm.) to that which can be logically inferred from that knowledge (Therefore she is not here in Chapel.). If this-then this. Yet Tom Long notes that sometimes, logic may move in the other direction, with the proof offered, not at the *beginning* of the chain, but at the *end*. "Sometimes such arguments do not move *from* what we know, but *toward* it," says Long.[2] We say, "If your roommate is asleep in the dorm, then she was not wandering about the campus looking for a good time on Sunday, therefore she is not at the Chapel."

But suppose you answer, "But she *is* in Chapel. She's singing in the choir. I see her. I said that our phone number is 555-9199, not 555-9192." See? Here the logic moves in a counter direction. She is not in the dorm because we experience her here in Chapel, there singing in the choir. This logic moves from what we don't know for sure back to what we know for certain, rippling back toward affirmation.

Thus, reasons Paul:

> If there is no resurrection of the dead . . .
> then Christ has not been raised.
> And if Christ has not been raised . . .
> then our preaching was a lie.
> And if our preaching was a lie . . .
> then your faith is futile.

At this point, I think Paul expected the gathered Corinthians to shout in unison, "But our faith is *not* futile." The Corinthians may have had problems with love (1 Corinthians 13), with getting along with one another in the church, but they had faith—spoke in tongues, worried about eating meat offered to idols, had knock-down drag-outs over baptism. They were just chock full of faith. Nobody could argue over their experience of Easter. Paul implies that the Corinthians were so full of faith, so dazzled by the Resurrection that, when he preached to them, he was forced to preach Jesus Christ and him crucified in an attempt to get them back down to earth for a few moments. Anybody who worshipped at one of their Sunday evening free-for-alls might go away thinking that Christians were weird, out of control, but nobody could deny that some life-giving power had been unleashed among them.

So let's reverse the order:

> Because your faith is *not* futile,
> Our preaching was not a lie,
> Christ has been raised,
> There is resurrection of the dead.

"Because your faith is not futile. . . . There is resurrection of the dead." It's an important truth. Easter begins to dawn, not in the preacher's assembling alleged "evidence" from history. The dry reconstruction of historians will not get us to resurrection. Easter begins in the recognition that our faith is not futile, in our present experience of the Risen Christ roaming among us. It is the testimony, not just of preachers like me, but of countless believers like you, that is the evidence. When bread and wine touch your lips and you see, feel the real presence. When you thought your heart would break in disappointment and pain, but it didn't because he was standing beside you in the dark. When you didn't know what to say and there were just the right words, words not of your own devising, being spoken by you. When you dragged into the church, cold at heart, skeptical, and distant, yet at the hymns your spirit rose to greet his, your faith is not in vain. This is the logic of Easter.

Sometimes the best sermons do not argue the congregation into something they have not yet known but rather point to and name that which the congregation undeniably knows. Having undeniably experienced resurrection, we now talk about it. Because your faith is not in vain, an Easter sermon is no lie, and Jesus is raised, therefore you are raised.

In the story of the first Easter (Luke 24:1-12) when the despondent women went out to the cemetery to pay their last respects to dead Jesus, they were surprised to find the tomb empty, shocked by the bright messengers who proclaimed, "He is not here. He has been raised."

Then, after this weird, frightening, wonderful experience, Luke says, "Then [the women] remembered his words. . ." (Luke 24:8). See? They moved from their strange but undeniable experience of Easter to remembered scriptural words about Easter.

And so have most of us.

Paul says that, without resurrection, there is nothing to preach (1 Corinthians 15:14).

Resurrection is presented in the Gospels and the letters of Paul as an experienced fact, that is, though we may have trouble grasping this datum, it is a datum nevertheless, a fact that is external to the constructs of our imagination, an experience that is neither of our making nor at our disposal but which invades human reality, changing our destiny. The risen Christ meets us, and then we attempt to bring that meeting to speech. The modern notion that resurrection is a projection of human longing, an inward experience of the believer, knows no basis in scripture. Resurrection is the supreme instance not of the fertile imaginings of our inner subjectivity but of the initiative and the active subjectivity of God who comes to us. If we were imagining a god and wishfully projecting something for which we had hoped, it is safe to say that we would not have imagined this God and Christ's resurrection. We are certainly capable of projecting much more docile, acceptable, and comfortable gods than the living, difficult, and demanding God we got in the Resurrection!

Christian preaching has its birth at Easter in that first astonished, breathless cry, "He is risen!" In a sense, this is as far as faithful preaching goes. As Paul says, without the Resurrection we literally have nothing to say and our preaching is in vain and our faith as well. The angel's word was not, "Jesus is raised, now you will all get to see your loved ones in eternity," though that eventually became an implication of the Resurrection. Rather, the angel's command was, "Go, tell!"

That which makes preaching specifically *Christian* preaching is that it is not only a description but also an active participation in the cross and resurrection, the defeat and victory of Jesus. To be faithful to the cross-resurrection, the Lent-Easter dynamic, something must die, must become silent as the awesome silence of Good Friday, must confess despair and give up, and then must announce and proclaim that something has happened, a miracle from God has come upon us, unexpected, undeserved, and undesired. He is risen!

Paul told the Corinthians to consider themselves, to look at their own radically transformed situation. They were once nothing, strangers separated by a host of divisions; now they are something, family, first wave of the new age, God's great movement to reclaim the world. God "has chosen things low and contemptible, mere nothings, to overthrow the existing order" (1 Corinthians 1:28 NEB). In our preaching, God uses a frail, lowly human being to accomplish divine work, even as was accomplished in the cross and resurrection.

What happens in preaching is something theologically akin to what happens in Christ as displayed in Paul's kenosis hymn in Philippians 2:

> Have this mind among yourselves, which is yours in Christ Jesus, who, though he was in the form of God, did not count equality with God a thing to be grasped, but emptied himself, taking the form of a servant, being born in the likeness of men. And being found in human form he humbled himself and became obedient unto death, even death on a cross. Therefore God has highly exalted him and bestowed on him the name which is above every name, that at the name of Jesus every knee should bow, in heaven and on earth and under the earth, and every tongue confess that Jesus Christ is Lord, to the glory of God the Father. (Philippians 2:5-11 RSV)

Christian preaching can't stop with the cross. To do so leads to a morbid kind of preaching that merely wallows in suffering and guilt, almost gleefully notes the abundant evidence of injustice and evil in the world, and then predictably urges some form of human action to right the wrongs that ail us. Insufferable moralism characterizes so much preaching because it never gets beyond the, "Look what we did to Jesus and still do to one another. We ought to do better." Filling the air with "should," "ought," and "must," moralistic preaching elevates Law over Gospel and transforms the good news of what God has done and is doing in the Resurrection into the bad news of an exhortation. Since God has not acted decisively, we must try harder. Anthropology replaces theology and self-salvation is the theme.

Or separation of the cross from resurrection can also lead to mindless "praise" in which, all evidence to the contrary, we praise, praise, praise for nothing. Stiff upper lip, put a happy face on the world, keep working and wishing, and move forward in celebration of ourselves and our potential. Truly Christian praise is reflexive, responsive to what God has done and is doing. The fitting response to the extravagant proclamation, "Jesus Christ is raised!" is invariably, "Hallelujah!"

The Resurrection is about God, about God's amazing ability finally to get what God wants, about God's ultimate triumph over our sin and our death. We read all scripture backward, back from the final chapter, as a story of the eventual triumph of God. Knowing how the story ends, knowing full well that God will eventually get God's way with the world, we do not lose hope. Easter is the promise that God will not leave us to our own devices, will not be defeated by us. Easter is the firm assurance that God will get what God wants.

So if preaching fails and fails often, preaching also, by the grace of God, succeeds. Despite all obstacles and hindrances, people do hear. A new world is created on the basis of nothing but the words. A new people, a church, are evoked out of nothing more than God's ability to work wonders through our preaching. Preachers are therefore powerful people because God has chosen to use preaching to bring to nothing things that the world regards as something and to bring to something things that the world regards as nothing.

If there is one thing we preachers fear more than the possibility of crucifixion it is the potential of resurrection. Failure in preaching can eventually be accepted, but success in preaching is a summons, an assignment, a kind of scary disruption. Over the years, I have noted that if there is one thing we preachers fear more than not being heard it is being heard, being part of God's movement into the world, dying and rising, giving birth, rebirth, liberating a life, being a vessel of the Holy Spirit, watching resurrection when it happens right before our very eyes.

One of the greatest challenges of Christian preaching is working with the Risen Christ. It would be one thing to preach about the subject of Christ, but "We preach Christ" crucified and resurrected (1 Corinthians 1:21-23). We do not preach ideas, precepts, principles but a living, active, resourceful person, Jesus Christ. Our challenge is well represented by the movements of the risen Christ in John 20. It is "the first day of the week," that is the first day of the Jewish work week, the first day when Israel, including the disciples of Jesus, are attempting to get back to normal after a particularly bloody weekend. Unfortunately, the yearning to get back to business will be disrupted by the Resurrection. He will appear among them, kick open their locked doors, and speak to them, command and commission them, and then disappear from them, moving on, alluding their grasp.

The call of Paul the apostle was his experience of finding himself living in a whole new world. He changed because of his realization that, in Jesus Christ, the world had changed. It was not merely that he discovered a new way of describing the world but rather that his citizenship had been moved to a radically transformed world. Paul's key testimonial to this recreation is in his Second Letter to the Corinthians:

> So if anyone is in Christ, there is a new creation: everything old has passed away; see, everything has become new! All this is from God, who reconciled us to himself through Christ, and has given us the ministry of reconciliation. (2 Corinthians 5:17-18)

Verse 17, in the Greek, lacks both subject and verb, so it is best rendered by the exclamatory, "If anyone is in Christ—new creation!"

Certainly, old habits die hard. There are still, as Paul acknowledges so eloquently in Romans 8, "the sufferings of this present time." The resistance and outright rejection that preachers suffer is evidence that the church has not yet fully appreciated the eschatological, end-of-the-age, transformed arrangements that ought to characterize the church. We always preach between the times, and rejection is often a sign that the old age and the principalities and powers still run rampant.

That many of us preachers still preach using essentially secular (i.e., godless) means of persuasion borrowed uncritically from the world is yet another testimony to our failure to believe that God raised Jesus Christ from the dead, thus radically changing everything. In so doing, we act as if Jesus were still sealed securely in the tomb, as if he did not come back to us, did not speak to us and cannot, will not speak to us today, as if preaching is something that we do through our strategies rather than through the speaking of the risen Christ.

Resurrection is not only the content of gospel preaching but also its miraculous means. Where two or three of us are gathered in his name, daring to talk about him, he is there, talking to us (Matthew 18:20). All the way to the end of the age, in every part of the world, in our baptism and proclamation, he is with us (Matthew 28:20).

I once heard a church growth expert declare, "Any church that doesn't have a pull-down video screen will be dead in ten years." But I believe that better technology does not make sermons work. Lack of technology cannot kill a church. Only God can kill a church. Only a living Christ can make our sermons speak to a new generation.

Christian preaching can never rest on my human experience or even on the experience of the oppressed, as some forms of Liberation Theology attempt to do, because human experience tends to be limited by the world's deadly, deathly means of interpretation. The world keeps telling Christians to "get real," to "face facts," but we have—after the cross and resurrection—a very particular opinion of what is real. I don't preach Jesus' story in the light of my experience, as some sort of helpful symbol or myth that is helpfully illumined by my own story of struggle and triumph. Rather, I am invited by Easter to interpret my story in the light of God's triumph in the Resurrection. I really don't have a story, I don't know the significance of my little life until I read my story and view my life through the lens of the cross and res- urrection. One of the things that occurs in the weekly preaching of the gospel is to lay the gospel story over our stories and reread our lives in the light of what is real now that crucified Jesus has been raised from the dead.

So last week, when I was in conversation with a troubled soul in my congregation and was asked by him, "Preacher, do you really think that I can ever get a grip on my addiction to heroin?" I almost responded, "No. Almost no one ever gets that monkey off his back. I really don't think you can get better." But then I remem- bered that we are in the Great Fifty Days of Easter, that time when the church, in its liturgical wisdom, keeps insisting that we tell the story of the resurrection of Christ as our story, as a truthful account of what is really going on in the world. So I responded, "You know, if this were about you or even the two of us working together, the answer is 'No, you can't get better.' Fortunately, in the afterglow of Easter, this is about God, about God's determination to free you and to give you the life God intends for you. Now that Jesus has been raised from the dead, there's always hope for us."

Only because we worship a resurrected Lord can we risk preaching. Our claims for preaching have little to do with a savvy utilization of various contemporary rhetorical insights; rather our claims arise from our very peculiar theological convictions about a very particular God who, in the cross and resurrection, is vastly different from any god we know.

The essential patience required of preachers, the freedom from homiletical anxiety over the reaction of our listeners, the confi- dence in the power of the preached word to accomplish what it wants, is possible only if, in fact, Jesus did rise from the tomb.

As Rowan Williams says,

> The Christian proclamation of the resurrection of the crucified just man, his return to his unfaithful friends and his empowering of them to forgive in his name offers a paradigm of the "saving"

process; yet not only a paradigm. It is a story which is itself an indispensable agent in the completion of this process, because it witnesses to the one personal agent in whose presence we may have full courage to "own" ourselves as sinners and full hope for a humanity whose identity is grounded in a recognition and affirmation by nothing less than God. It is a story which makes possible the comprehensive act of *trust.* . . .[3]

Sometimes we preachers are tempted to play God, to fill up all the gaps between Jesus and our people, to bypass the need for a Holy Spirit, to make Christ too easily available to them, to dumb down discipleship so that anyone can wander in off the street and get it without cost, risk, or conversion. We are so desperate to be heard and accepted on our own terms, so desperate to find a way to preach the gospel without recourse to the power of God in the living Christ. But "stewards of the mysteries of God" (1 Corinthians 4:1) ought not be too free in dispensing and disposing of the mystery that is Christ. There is no way from here to there, no path from heaven to earth, from death to life, except the one that God makes. We ought to preach in such a way that, if Jesus has not been raised from the dead, then our sermons are utterly incomprehensible. Faithful sermons require the presence of the Holy Spirit to make them work. If Jesus has not been raised from the dead and has not returned to us to resume the conversation, then we preachers ought to fall flat on our face.

It makes a world of difference whether or not a preacher has been encountered by the living, speaking, resurrected Christ. Thus, making doxology to God (Romans 11:33-36), Paul asks that we present ourselves as "a living sacrifice, holy and acceptable to God" by not being "conformed to this world" but by being "transformed by the renewing of your minds" (Romans 12:1-2). All of this is resurrection talk, the sort of tensive situation of those who find their lives still in an old, dying world yet also are conscious of a new world being born. Our lives are eschatologically stretched between the sneak preview of the new world being shown to us in the church and the old world where the principalities and powers are reluctant to give way. We throw out our frail voices into a dying world and they come back to us, in the lives of those in the congregation who have seen and heard the risen Christ and who now embody that new life in their lives.

As pastors, we see a world in the grip of the enemy, the final enemy, but we also, by the grace of God, get to see the enemy losing his grip upon some of the territory he once thought was his. We see death and the cross being raised again in a thousand places but we also see Jesus. In the meantime, which is the only time the church has ever known, we live as those who know something about the fate of the world that the world does not yet know, something so grand and wonderful that we cannot keep silent. We must go and tell. We must preach.

Paul confesses his own internalization of the Resurrection in which he places Easter at the center of his discipleship:

> I want to know Christ and the power of his resurrection and the community of his sufferings by becoming just like him in his death, so that I might be like him in his resurrection. No, I have not already obtained such a state, nor have I already reached the goal; but I press on to make it my own, because Christ Jesus has made me his own. Sisters and brothers, I do not consider that I have already made this my own; but this one thing I do: forgetting what lies behind and straining forward toward what lies ahead, I press on toward the goal, the prize, the upward call of God in Jesus Christ. (Philippians 3:10-14 author paraphrase)

Because of Easter, we preachers are not permitted despair. We keep forgetting what is behind and straining forward, eager to see what else a risen Christ can do through our preaching. There is certainly enough failure and disappointment in the preaching life to understand why depression, disillusionment, and despair could be considered the three curses of the preaching ministry. Despair is most understandable among some of our most conscientious and dedicated preachers. Any pastor who is not tempted by despair has probably given in to the world too soon, has become dishonest and deceitful about his or her homiletical failures, has become too easily pleased by and accommodated to present arrangements, is expecting too little of the preached word. Weekly confrontation with the gap between what God dares to say to us and what we are able to hear, leads many of our best and brightest to despondency. We grieve for the church, and we despair that preaching really is as effective as God promises it to be. It seems sometimes as if our faith is in vain and our preaching is in vain. It seems as if God's Word returns to God empty.

Yet, as Paul says, after the resurrection of Christ we do not grieve as those who have no hope. If our hope were in ourselves or our techniques for the skillful and effective proclamation of the gospel, we might well abandon hope. Our hope is in Christ, who for reasons known only fully to himself, has determined our spoken words to be a major means of his powerful presence in the world. Many Sundays I do not know why, and many Sundays, standing at the door of the church, bidding farewell to the worshippers, I see no evidence for Christ's faith in us preachers. The congregation appears to have heard nothing, and the world seems sadly the same.

Yet by the grace of God, I do so believe. I do believe that we have something to preach, and I do believe that we preachers work not alone. In Jesus Christ, God is reconciling the world to himself. And Easter tells us that God's purposes shall not be defeated, not by the Enemy, nor death, nor principalities and powers, nor even by the church itself.

There is that sort of homiletical despair that leads some of our brothers and sisters to quit, to stop talking and to go into less demanding vocations. Yet there is also that despair, which I find more widespread, that leads some of us to slither into permanent cynicism about the efficacy of preaching.

"Preaching doesn't change people," becomes their mantra.

Some of this sense of the vanity of preaching is due to lack of faith that God can do any new thing with us. It is sad to see such accommodation to sin and death. How do we know that Easter is not true? Who told us that Jesus used bad judgment when he made us his witnesses to the Resurrection even to the ends of the earth?

In order for the powers-that-be to have their way with us, to convince us that the rumor of resurrection is a lie, they must first convince us that death is "reality" and that wisdom comes in uncomplaining adjustment to that reality—"This is it. This is all there is. Preaching is woefully archaic, one-sided, authoritarian indoctrination that is bound to fail. Get used to it."

If one considers the evidence for the resurrection of Jesus—the birth of the church from the once despondent and defeated disciples, the perseverance of the saints even unto today, last Sunday's sermon that changed a life—it is difficult to see why anyone would disbelieve it, except for two reasons:

1. The Resurrection is an odd occurrence, outside the range of our usual experience, so that makes it difficult for our conceptual abilities. We tend to reject that which we lack the conceptual apparatus for understanding. Because we cannot conceive of resurrection, we deny its possibility.

2. Perhaps more important, if Jesus is raised from the dead, if the Resurrection is true, a fact that is real, then we must change. Resurrection carries with it a claim, a demand that we live in the light of this stunning new reality or else appear oddly out of step. Now we must acknowledge who sits upon the throne, who is in charge, how the story ends. Now we must either change, join in God's revolution, or else remain unchanged, in the grip of the old world and its rulers, sin and death.

Thus because we preachers must, at least on a yearly basis, preach resurrection, we keep being challenged to live and talk in the light of the Resurrection. We keep being born again into a new reality. We are not permitted the old excuse for lethargy, "People don't change." Certainly, everything we know about people suggests that they usually don't change. But sometimes they do. And that keeps us preachers nervous and sitting lightly on our cynicism. Change is rare, virtually impossible, were it not that Jesus has been raised from the dead. When a pastor keeps working with some suffering parishioner, even when there is no discernible change in that person's life, when a pastor keeps preaching the truth even with no visible congregational response, that pastor is being a faithful witness to the resurrection (Luke 1:2). That preacher is continuing to be obedient to the charge of the angel at the tomb to go and tell something that has changed the fate of the world (Matthew 28:7), which the world cannot know if no one dares to tell.

Preacher Paul was not only the great missionary to the Gentiles but also living proof that the dead can be raised, thus accounting for his frequently self-referential testimonials of his encounter with Christ. In Paul's encounter, the dead Jesus was not only seen as raised but the Church Enemy Number One, Paul, was also raised. On Easter, Jesus was not just raised from the dead. He did not just return to us, he returned to *us*, to the very ones who had so forsaken and denied him. When he appeared first and most frequently to his own disciples (the ones who, when the soldiers came to arrest him, had fled into the darkness) the risen Christ thereby demonstrated that it is of the nature of the true and living God to forgive. And not only to forgive but also to call, commission, and commandeer. "Go! Tell!"

Easter keeps differentiating the church from a respectable, gradually progressive, moral improvement society. Here, there are sudden lurches to the left and to the right, falling backward and lunging forward, people breaking loose and getting out of control. Easter keeps reminding us pastors that the church is the result of something that God in Jesus Christ has done, not something we have done. When the world wants change, the world raises an army, arms itself to the teeth, and marches forth with banners unfurled to storm the wilderness. When the God of the cross and resurrection wants to change the world, this God always does so nonviolently, through some voice crying in the wilderness, through preaching.

Easter is great grace to those well-disciplined, hard-working, conscientious preachers who are so often in danger of thinking that the kingdom of God depends mostly on their well-constructed and energetically delivered sermons. Easter is also a warning to cautious and too prudent preachers that they ought to expect to live on the edge, ought not to expect to be "kept" by the church. A resurrected Christ is pure movement, elusive, evasive, he goes ahead of us, will not be held by us. A true and living God seems to enjoy shocking and surprising those who think that they are tight with God. We therefore ought to press the boundaries of what is possible and what is impossible to say in the pulpit, ought to keep working the edges as if miracles were not miraculous at all but simply typical of a God who loves to raise the dead. We ought to preach in such a reckless, utterly-dependent-upon-God sort of way that if God has not vindicated the peculiar way of Jesus by raising him from the dead then our ministry is in vain. But, as Paul says, thank God, our faith in resurrection is not in vain because, by the grace of God, our preaching is not in vain.

CHAPTER SIX

THE POLITICAL WORD

When Jesus was born, according to Luke, the powerful people, the powerful political people up at the palace, missed it. The *angeloi*, the heavenly messengers from God came to none of them. Rather, the heavens split open, songs filled the air, and an angelic army appeared to poor shepherds out in the fields working the night shift. That's strange.

Even more strange was what the angels said. "Glory to God in the highest heaven, and on earth peace among those whom he favors!" The phrase on the angels' lips is an almost direct quote from the opening lines of the decrees of Caesar Augustus, one of the world's most effective dictators. When some imperial decree was made by the Caesar's occupation forces in the Near East to those who dwelt out in the provinces, this was how it began: "Glory to the most august Caesar (otherwise known as God in the Highest), and peace on earth to those with whom god Augustus is well pleased"—the implication being that there will be hell to pay for those with whom god Augustus is not pleased.

See? Luke has put the imperialist words of Augustus on the lips of the angels. When Jesus was born in Bethlehem, there was a royal decree: There's a new King on the throne. Jesus Christ is King. Therefore, neither Augustus nor anybody else is King.

A Baptist campus minister from Mississippi brought a group of students through town and asked me to meet with them. They were college students on their way to do some good Baptist work among the poor in Appalachia.

During our conversation, this kid, with a baseball cap turned wrong way on his head, asked, "What do you do as a Christian when people really get mad at you and want to hurt you because you're a Christian?"

I said that I wasn't exactly sure to what he was alluding. With more than a touch of sarcasm in my voice I said to him, "Being a Methodist, we have managed to rework the gospel in such a way that nobody could ever draw ire or get hurt being a Christian! I'm always so nice about Jesus that nobody has ever tried to crucify me; what exactly do you mean?"

He said, "Well, for instance, the other night we were talking about the war with Iraq after our fraternity meeting. Most everybody thought the president knew what he was doing, that the war was a good thing, that a preemptive strike was justified. All I said was that I thought the war was a very bad idea. I'm a Christian. That's not how we think the world is set up. That's not how we handle evil. Besides, I'm a Baptist, and we tend to always be suspicious of the government, no matter who's in charge.

"That was when they started yelling at me. Told me if I didn't like living in America I ought to go someplace else. Called me names, even."

Now there's a kid who's got a strange notion of who's in charge, who sits on the throne. Where did he get the notion that George W. is not in charge? There is no way, I submit, that he could have gotten this news about a new world except through the preaching of sermons in his little Baptist church in Mississippi.

When Karl Barth wrote the Barmen Declaration, whereby the Confessing Church stood up to Hitler's German Christians and their easy syncretism of Nazism and Christianity, Barth defied Hitler on the basis of an appeal to the church's need to preach the gospel no matter who was in power in government. Barth said in the Barmen Declaration that the best way for the church to serve the needs of the world was through the free, undeterred preaching of the gospel. No one, not Hitler, nor anybody else could keep the church from its homiletical service to Jesus

Christ, "as the one Word of God which we have to hear and which we have to trust and obey in life and in death."

The church does not often indulge in political preaching but rather, simply by its preaching, the church is "political." All politics is, at least incipiently, a claim about to whom we ought to listen and obey in life and in death. Preaching cannot be faithful Christian preaching without at the same time being "political."

Sometime ago, a man, a layperson in a large church in the Midwest, at the conclusion of my lecture on preaching, said to me, "The trouble with you preachers is that you just don't speak my language. You don't say anything that relates to my world."

He meant it as damning criticism, I'm sure. I replied, in love, "Where in the world would you get the notion that I, or any of my pastoral sisters and brothers, would want to speak in your language or to your world? I don't want to speak to your world. I want to rock your world! I want to give you a new language that you wouldn't know without my preaching. I want to destroy your world and offer you another. I'm a preacher, for God's sake!"

For God's sake, we preachers wade into perilous waters, perilous not only because human beings have a propensity toward self-deceit and evasion of the truth but also because they are waters that have been stirred up and troubled by a living, resurrected Christ.

I heard a preacher say, at a gathering of us preachers, "I never want to cause division or dissension in one of my sermons. I believe in the ministry of reconciliation, the ministry of encouragement. Christ has called me to be a peacemaker."

I thought, upon hearing this preacher's self-declared call for a homiletics of reconciliation, that if he never wants dissension and trouble in the congregation, he surely must never preach from the Bible. Scripture appears to have as its intent the provocation of, or at least ministry to, conflict rather than the avoidance of all conflict. Again, preaching that is biblical does not simply want to speak to the modern world but rather wants to move people to a different world, a world that would have been unavailable to them without our preaching.

Luther compares the preaching of the Word of God to the use of a sharp scalpel by a surgeon and says that the preacher "should not be silent or mumble but should testify without being frightened or bashful. He should speak out candidly without regarding or sparing anyone, let it strike whomever or whatever it will. It is a great hindrance to a preacher if he looks around and worries about what people like or do not like to hear. . . ."[1] Luther recalls that Ambrosius, after admonishing his congregation to come hear a good sermon was told, "The truth is, dear pastor, that if you were to tap a keg of beer in church and call us to enjoy it, we would be glad to come."[2] Our people and their opinions are interesting for us preachers but never ultimately interesting because we preachers are sinners preaching to sinners who are always reluctant to let go of the security and stability of the old order.

Faithful biblical preaching seeks not just agreement from the hearers but rather conversion, a shift of power and a transference of authority, nothing less than death and resurrection. All faithful Christian preaching is in this sense "political," because it always involves a dispute over just who is in charge of our world and therefore of our lives.

Therefore faithful preaching is always more than a mild-mannered artful description of the world and the human condition. It must also be part of a process of conversion. In order to enter this strange Kingdom of Heaven, we must be born again, and again, and again. And there is rarely any truly painless birth. In order for something to be born, it must die. An old world must give way for a new one to be born. People generally do not let go of their old, predictable world without a fight. So preaching without conflict is a theological impossibility.

In the middle of his commentary on Isaiah, the prophet-poet-preacher Martin Luther exclaims, "How difficult an occupation preaching is. Indeed, to preach the Word of God is nothing less than to bring upon oneself all the furies of hell and of Satan, and therefore also of . . . every power of this world. It is the most dangerous kind of life to throw oneself in the way of Satan's many teeth."[3]

Satan does not give up territory easily, showing his many teeth whenever his rule is threatened. Preaching seeks to convert people, to move them from where they are to where God intends for them to be. Thus preaching cannot avoid being "political," cannot avoid asserting who rules, who is in charge, who sits upon the throne, and therefore preaching cannot avoid conflict. To hear the gospel is to wake up and to realize that one is living in a different world now that Jesus Christ has claimed a kingdom and formed a people. Preaching is an announcement of the reality of the reign of God. To be sure, the complete sovereignty of God is not yet fully established. But it is on its way and is a present reality wherever anyone dares to stand up and dispute the world's delusions with the cry, "Jesus Christ is Lord." Preaching must not simply state the present situation with accuracy and empathy; it must seek to move, to redeem, to detoxify and to convert, to free people from that which enslaves them. Their liberation begins in our proclamation, with our statement of who is in charge, who sits on the throne, who reigns. In Romans 10:15, Paul makes an allusion to Isaiah 52 that makes clear that preaching is a proclamation meant to end a dispute over just who is in charge:

> How beautiful upon the mountains
>   are the feet of him who brings good tidings,
> who publishes peace, who brings good tidings of good,
>   who publishes salvation,
> who says to Zion, "Your God reigns."
> (Isaiah 52:7 RSV)

Thus preaching to be truly Christian can never be safely personal, subjective, and individual (the way the world would like to limit our speaking to mere therapy and respectful dialogue rather than pushy proclamation). Preaching originates in a God who when God "utters his voice, the earth melts" (Psalm 46:6). Preaching must be social, cosmic, and political. A wide-ranging, earth-shattering claim is being made in our preaching. "For our struggle is not against enemies of blood and flesh, but against the rulers, against the authorities, against the cosmic powers of this present darkness, against the spiritual forces of evil in the heavenly places" (Ephesians 6:12).

When Jesus met someone enslaved by an "evil spirit," he went head-to-head with evil. How? He rebuked the spirit by confronting the powers with nothing but the Word. He pronounced the evil spirit null and impotent and announced the sovereignty of God over this person's life. Then Jesus commanded the unclean spirit to "be silent" (Luke 4:35).

To be a preacher is to be willing to assert that the powers are not in power, to be willing to engage in critique, rebuke, and talk that is counter to the way the world talks. Daily, relentlessly, people are bombarded by the lies and the false speech of a myriad of voices, most of them commercially, technologically delivered. Those voices must be rebuked, silenced, so that God can talk and be heard and be loved and be obeyed.

Although it is questionable how often a sermon ought to be used for political advice-giving and diatribe (we don't want to give too much credence to the powers, and our time is limited in a sermon to more important matters than secular politics), all faithful sermons are inescapably "political" in that they are always a claim about who is really in charge and therefore, by implication, part of a formation of a *polis*, a people who act and talk differently from the world. Therefore preaching is not only an exercise in the theological category of justification—the reconciliation of humanity to God, conversion, being born again, saved by grace. Preaching is also the practice of sanctification— God's gracious equipment, formation, and inculcation of that reconciliation in believers' lives by the continuing formative work of the Holy Spirit through the ministrations of the church. In preaching, people not only hear an announcement of their changed situation (justification) but also are given a new language and a new grammar whereby they are enabled daily to participate in that new world (sanctification). As a preacher describes what God has done in Jesus Christ, people are being formed into a new people by water and the Word.

Luke 4:16-30, Jesus' abortive sermon in his hometown synagogue in Nazareth stands as constant warning to us preachers and to our congregations. Preaching has to do not simply with our words but with the Word of God, a Word intruding into our settled arrangements, a Word not of our own concoction. To be the recipient of that Word is sometimes to be in pain because of it. As Luther said, here is a Word that first kills in order to make alive, that damns in order to bless. Preaching is something akin to surgery.

Kierkegaard noted that so many people have become famous and prosperous by making modern people's lives easier, inventing labor-saving devices, enabling people to live more comfortably. He said that he felt called to make peoples' lives more difficult and painful. Therefore, he felt called to be a preacher, a servant of the truth.[4]

Through preaching, the Word of God keeps growing, multiplying, leaping over all boundaries (Song of Songs 2:8; Acts 19:20). Our contemporary proclamation is not a lecture about the Word of God; rather the church has testified, on the basis of its own experience, that *"Praedicatio verbi dei est verbum dei"* (to encounter preaching is to encounter God). God graciously allows the words of us poor preachers to be, in the action of the Holy Spirit, the very Word of God.

An illuminating episode occurs in Acts 17. By this time in the Acts of the Apostles, Luke has taken Paul to a variety of situations where he has spoken eloquently to the power of the gospel. But can the gospel hold its own in a sophisticated university town? Luke brings Paul to Athens, the cradle of classical civilization, the city of the art of Pericleites and Phidias. Frankly, Paul is unimpressed. Good Jew that he is, he sees Athens as a wasteland "full of idols" (17:16). Paul sees idolatry everywhere. So he does a very Jewish thing. He initiates conflict. "He argued in the synagogue with the Jews . . . and also in the marketplace every day . . . Also some Epicurean and Stoic philosophers debated with him" (17:17-18). Many mock what Paul has to say, but some, the more open-minded among them, ask him to speak in their Areopagus because they mistakenly believe that he is presenting a "new teaching" (v. 19), even though Paul has been testifying, rather laboriously throughout his previous speeches in Acts, that the gospel is not an innovation but rather the fulfillment of God's historic promises to Israel.

This gives Luke the opportunity to depict Paul as a great classical speaker, putting on his lips one of the most perfectly formed of classical orations, conforming perfectly to Aristotle's concepts of a good speech. In earlier sermons in Acts, Paul has cited much Scripture. But this sermon is to a group of pagans, so he uncharacteristically begins by basing his argument on a sort of natural theology, adapting his presentation to the limits of his pagan audience.

Aristotle advised winning the trust of one's audience early in the speech. Is that what Paul does when he begins, "'Athenians, I see how extremely religious you are in every way. For as I went through the city and looked carefully at the objects of your worship, I found among them an altar with the inscription, "To an unknown god"'" (17:22-23)? Or is Paul, good Jew that he is, saying something to the effect, "I see how extremely religious and spiritual you are" (not necessarily a Jewish compliment); "I've seen some idolatry in my time, but I think you have more idols in this place than anywhere else I've visited. I noticed that you even have an altar to a god whom you don't know. You are ready to worship that god before you even know its name. You've never seen an idol you couldn't bow before."

Whether Paul is praising their groping after the divine (17:27) or criticizing their credulous idolatry, I do not know. He cites "some of your own poets" (17:28) and our common humanity (17:26), perhaps using a bit of natural theology on them. But then Paul moves to a claim for which there is no natural evidence in nature, no commonsensical access. Paul speaks of one who shall judge the world in righteousness (17:31), one who was vindicated by being raised from the dead. Having lowered their guard by implying that they have access to the divine through their present experience, Paul inserts that for which there is no prior human experience—judgment and resurrection. These eschatological realities determine the limits of a Christian appeal to human experience, for they reveal a content of Christian proclamation that can only be had as a gift of God, not by our experientially based efforts.

Reaction of the crowd is reminiscent of some of the reaction to Peter's speech at Pentecost in Acts 2. "When they heard of the resurrection of the dead, some scoffed . . . " says Luke (Acts 2 17:32). At that point church is out. Only a few are converted and born again—Dionysius and a woman named Damaris (Acts 17:34). These are rather modest results for one of the most perfectly formed speeches, one of the only classically rhetorical speeches, in the New Testament.

The meager response is proof that Christian communicators like Paul have a problem. They may try to build upon people's common experiences of the world and nature. They may establish links with their culture. Yet at some point, the faithful Christian communicator must cite revelation, must put forth that knowledge that does not arise from human experience but rather as a gift, must risk conflict, dissension, misunderstanding, and rejection. Apostles are defined in Acts as "witnesses to the resurrection" (see Acts 1:21-22). When the resurrection is preached, apostles risk mocking and communicative dissonance. Ultimately, Christian communication like preaching is not based upon human experience or upon skillful oral presentation. Preaching is a gift of a God who is graciously self-revealing. I have therefore in this book noted repeatedly the theological claim that preaching "works" because this God intends to speak, to make contact with a beloved, still-being-redeemed creation. The one "who hears you hears me" (Luke 10:16). Many a failure of preaching is due not to the poor talents of the preacher but to the difficulty of the gospel, the strangeness of hearing tell of a world upheld by the one in whom we live and move and have our being, a God who is quite different from the art and imagination of humanity. We fail because, in our preaching, it is as if we are talking about a different world.

Because preaching is a gift of God, it is prone to failure, as the paltry results of Paul's sermon at Athens prove. Because we are sinful creatures whose hearing, like our other capacities, is perverted, preaching quite often falls upon deaf ears. Yet the miracle of it all is that, by the grace of God, people do hear the voice of God in our preaching. They call it the Acts of the Apostles, but they might as well have called it the Acts of the Holy Spirit, or even the Acts of the Holy Spirit through Apostolic Preaching. Nothing, says Acts, can defeat the Word that is empowered through the Holy Spirit. The last word of the Acts of the Apostles is a key to the entire book—"unhindered" (Acts 28:31 RSV). Nothing can hinder the Word.

So preachers must combine realism about the limits of preaching with realism about the power of the Holy Spirit to effect the hearing it deserves. While preaching places a large intellectual burden upon both preachers and hearers, we preachers must not underestimate the huge political demand we are placing upon our hearers in our preaching. We are doing nothing less than inviting them to move to another world. Pastors are sometimes frustrated by the lack of congregational response to their sermons. Yet, as Paul noted in one of his congregations, we plant the seed, nurture the soil, but it is up to God to give the harvest. Faithful preaching is always more than a respectful conversation between the gospel and the world as we have received it. Though it is that preaching is also confrontation, assault, announcement, and collision with the received world, all of which can be painful.

Yet because of the political challenge of Christian preaching, because of all the strong forces arrayed against the hearing of the word in Athens, Greece, or Athens, Georgia, or anywhere else, it is all the more amazing that people *do hear* the Word of God through our pitiful preaching, do encounter the risen Christ through our sorry sermons. Nothing finally can hinder that hearing. By the power of a living God, "The word of the Lord grew mightily and prevailed" (Acts 19:20). "The word of God increased, and the number of the disciples multiplied greatly . . . " (Acts 6:7 RSV). Unhindered.

As we have noted, Luke begins his story of Jesus by depicting an evening sky filled with angels as his first act in the story of *Jesus*. These *angeloi*, "angels," are heavenly heralds who bring politically charged "good news of salvation." The good news requires messengers, someone to come out and deliver the news. One of these messengers brought the news to Mary that she was going to have a baby and name him, "Emmanuel," God with Us.

The angel at that time clearly warned mother Mary that her baby was going to be a major cause of trouble for the world of Caesar and be a cause of much pain in order for there to be much blessing.

Yet after delivering the news, we hear very little of these heavenly messengers, these *angeloi*, these first preachers. They appear only briefly in a couple of places in Luke–Acts, usually when God is about to do something so very strange and impossible that God needs an angel sent down from heaven to tell the news. And when these angels do appear, sometimes we are told their names, but usually not. And we are told nearly nothing about them as individuals—their personalities, their antecedents, their gifts or concerns. It is as if these angels are made of gossamer, as if they appear, speak, deliver their message from God, and then disappear. It is as if they are transparent to the message that they are delivering, as if they are nothing except the word they deliver, as if they are pure speech. Their main significance is in no way in themselves but rather in the message they are given to speak.

In their transparency, in their significance being purely derivative of the message they are to speak, I take these angels, these messengers of good news, as prototypes and models of all Christian preachers who have ever been. These *angeloi* are all of us whose significance is subservient to the Word, whose life consists in what we are able to say in God's name, who have no other great purpose than preaching what we are told to say.

In a series of sermons on Ezekiel, Gregory the Great (c. 540–604) refers to these *angeloi*. Gregory hears the prophet speak of the "sound of wings like the sound of many waters." This leads Gregory into a digression upon the significance of God's angelic preachers, these "winged messengers" through which heaven does business with earth. The sound of their wings, bearing divine messages addressed to humanity, "at first gives out a small sound, issuing only from the saints." Only rarely do we read in scripture of a direct message from God delivered by a winged creature, for they are as yet few in number and their sound is slight. Yet eventually, in the story of the church and its preaching, that holy sound of angelic wings "is diffused over all by the ministry of preaching; it resonates through the conversion of many peoples."[5]

Gregory admits that, at the time of Christ's earthly ministry, "there were not many of these winged living beings our text speaks about. . . ." Yet after Christ's resurrection and the angel's appearance at the empty tomb commanding proclamation, there was an explosion of messengers all bearing the message of salvation. Great was the company of preachers, and through these preachers, the Word of God grew and multiplied. Gregory asks, "Who knows how many little ones, how many serious old men, how many strong youths, how many weak, simple people, how many converted sinners, how many elderly virgins have through faith, hope, and love taken flight toward heavenly realms. Behold the sound of the wings, which first came from but a few creatures, now resonates among many peoples; now many desiring a heavenly life take to flight. . . .It is well said, 'And I heard the sound of wings as the sound of many waters.'"[6]

By the grace of God, their sound has gone out, their words have been heard. Words have been given wings, and the good news has had its way with the world, even unto our day, forever and ever. Amen.

NOTES

Introduction

1. George Barna, *Marketing the Church: What They Never Taught You About Church Growth* (Colorado Springs: NavPress, 1988), 50.

1. The Preached Word Is the Word of God

1. Quoted by Richard P. Heitzenrater, "Wesley, John," in *Concise Encyclopedia of Preaching*, ed. William H. Willimon and Richard Lischer (Louisville: Westminster/John Knox, 1995), 500.

2. Quoted by Hughes Oliphant Old, *The Reading and Preaching of the Scriptures in the Worship of the Church* (Grand Rapids: Eerdmans, 2002), 4:11.

2. The Prophetic Word

1. Phillips Brooks, *Lectures on Preaching* (New York: E. P. Dutton & Company, 1907), 5.

2. Old, *Reading and Preaching of the Scriptures*, 4:20.

3. "Sermon on Matthew," in *Luther's Works*, ed. E. Plass (St. Louis: Concordia, 1959), III:1208.

4. Augustine, *Letters*, XXIX, To Alypius, A.D. 395, sections 6-8, in *A Select Library of the Nicene and Post-Nicene Fathers of the Christian Church*, ed. H. Wace and P. Schaff (New York: Christian, 1887), I:255.

5. Portions of this section are taken from William H. Willimon, *Pastor: The Theology and Practice of Ordained Leadership* (Nashville: Abingdon Press, 2000), 159ff.

6. Martin Luther, "The Freedom of a Christian," in *Martin Luther: Selections from His Writings*, by John Dillenberger (Garden City, N.Y.: Doubleday, 1961), 65.

7. P. T. Forsyth, *Positive Preaching and the Modern Mind* (New York: A. C. Armstrong, 1907), 71.

3. The Biblical Word

1. Karl Barth, *Homiletics*, trans. G. W. Bromiley and Donald E. Daniels (Louisville: Westminster/John Knox, 1991), 80.

2. Old, *Reading and Preaching of the Scriptures*, 2:258.

3. Some of the following material was taken from William H. Willimon, *Pastor: The Theology and Practice of Ordained Ministry* (Nashville: Abingdon Press, 2000), 54-95.

4. Walter Brueggemann, in *The Church as Counterculture*, ed. Michael L. Budde and Robert W. Brimlow (Albany: State University of New York, 2000), 53.

5. David H. Kelsey, *The Uses of Scripture in Recent Theology* (Philadelphia: Fortress Press, 1975), 90.

6. Stanley M. Hauerwas and William H. Willimon, *Resident Aliens: Life in the Christian Colony* (Nashville: Abingdon Press, 1989), 49.

7. Quoted in Old, *Reading and Preaching of the Scriptures*, 1:350.

8. Dietrich Bonhoeffer, *Life Together* (New York: Harper & Row, 1954), 97-98.

9. Walter Brueggemann, *Theology of the Old Testament: Testimony, Dispute, Advocacy* (Minneapolis: Fortress, 1997), 149.

4. The Incarnate Word

1. Dietrich Bonhoeffer, *Worldly Preaching*, ed. Clyde E. Fant (Nashville: Thomas Nelson, 1975), 129.

2. Ibid., 123.

3. Ibid., 126.

5. Cross and Resurrection in Preaching

1. Thomas G. Long, *The Senses of Preaching* (Atlanta: John Knox Press, 1988), 92-93.

2. Ibid., 44.

3. Rowan Williams, *Resurrection* (London: Darton, Longman & Todd, 1982), 49.

6. The Political Word

1. "The Sermon on the Mount," in *Luther's Works*, 21:9.

2. Quoted in Thomas C. Oden, *Ministry through Word and Sacrament* (New York: Crossroad, 1989), 2:32.

3. As quoted by Charles Campbell, "Resisting the Powers," in *Purposes of Preaching*, ed. Jana Childers (St. Louis: Chalice Press, 2004), 25.

4. From Charles E. Moore, ed., *Provocations: Spiritual Writings of Kierkegaard* (Farmington, Penn.: Plough Publishing House, 1999), 35.

5. Old, *Reading and the Preaching of the Scriptures*, 11:456-57.

6. Ibid.

INDEX OF NAMES

Index of Scripture